D1525034

THE STORY OF THE

TEXAS RANGERS

BY WALTER PRESCOTT WEBB

Illustrated by NICHOLAS EGGENHOFER
Preface by TERRELL WEBB

A BOULDIN HOUSE BOOK FROM THE ENCINO PRESS : AUSTIN

SECOND EDITION

PREFACE

WALTER PRESCOTT WEBB liked this book. He once told me that after he had written his earlier definitive history of The Texas Rangers, now published by The University of Texas Press, he could not resist the urge to type off some of these true stories of the Rangers in a more relaxed form. This book is the result of that urge.

He was in a position to know fact from fancy not only from the years of research into their history and his acquaintance and correspondence with the Rangers, but from his firsthand experience as a Texas Ranger. In August 1924, Dr. Webb says "Captain R. W. Aldrich took leave from his desk in Austin and we set out in a T model Ford for a tour of inspection of the Ranger camps. Adjutant General Thomas F. Barton issued me a Ranger commission while Captain Aldrich supplied the jewelry— a cartridge belt and a forty-five calibre Colt revolver. We took bedding and a chuck box preparatory to spending the entire time in the open." They were joined by Ranger J. A. (Arch) Miller of the Texas Big Bend and others. From Laredo they headed west along the Rio Grande. Walter Webb lived the life of the Texas Ranger, climaxing this unforgettable experience with rugged, close to the earth living near Boquillas in the Big Bend Country. They rode the rapids of the Rio Grande and did their sleeping on the ground. He was sinking his teeth into his Texas Ranger research. So, as a personal aside, it was with obvious delight that Dr. Webb accepted my suggestion that on our wedding trip following our marriage on December 14, 1961, we start at Brownsville and drive up the Rio Grande to the Big Bend National Park. This time it would be in an air-conditioned automobile and we would make stops along the way.

When we came to the end of our odyssey up in the Chisos Mountains, I was assured by my bridegroom guide that the brown and white goats we saw skipping up and down the canyon by the river were the same ones that had bleated at him thirty-seven years before. He took me to Castolon and to an out-post general store near Terlingua, where we had the same brand of crackers and cheese that he had remembered from that earlier expedition. It was a great experience for us both. I had the good fortune to listen to this Ranger historian, whose bride I had just become, tell some of his amazing stories. With our westward tour ended, we ate our Christmas Day dinner of chili and beans in Sanderson and drove straight east back to Austin.

It is with great pleasure that the Encino Press and I re-publish this true and uncomplicated *Story of the Texas Rangers*. It is designed for the general reader and is not fortified, embellished or encumbered, as the case may be, by footnotes, index or numerous statistics. In the larger definitive history, all that can be found.

TERRELL WEBB
Austin, 1971

CONTENTS

THE STORY OF THE TEXAS RANGERS

CHAPTER I

THE LEGEND OF COURAGE

THE small Texas town was held in a grip of fear. A mob was terrorizing the town, and nothing that the local authorities could do was any help in stopping it. Finally in desperation the mayor sent for the Texas Rangers. *They* would know how to cope with the situation.

Now the mayor and the loyal townspeople were lining the tracks waiting for the noon train to bring in the Ranger reinforcements. In the background the angry mob could be heard. When the train stopped, the people were in for a surprise, though. Off the train stepped a lone man. He had a sandy mustache, pale blue eyes, a Winchester in his hand, and a pistol in his belt.

The mayor approached the stranger and very cautiously asked, "Who are you?"

"I'm a Texas Ranger," the man answered quietly. In the distance the howl of the mob was getting louder.

"Where are your men?" asked the mayor.

"I am the only one," the Ranger replied.

"What! Only one Ranger? Why, man, we've got a mob! We need a company of Rangers!"

"You've only got one mob, haven't you?" The Ranger said calmly. "Let's go."

This never really happened, but you hear the story told everywhere that men meet to reminisce about the Texas Rangers. It is probably the most famous of all the legends which have grown up around this remarkable fighting force. Stories such as this have become true, because people have come to believe them to be true.

[1]

The legend of the Texas Rangers has been built from just such tales. The legend is one of unflinching courage, of the type which the single Ranger showed in the story. People came to expect the Rangers to live up to the legend, and this belief has affected the men who join the force, and has shaped their acts and their attitudes when they were part of it.

There is probably no group of fighting men on the American continent—or, perhaps in the whole world—which has made such a reputation. Begun in 1823, formally organized in 1835, the Rangers have existed for one and a quarter centuries. No fighting group can boast a more colorful history. As they made their reputation the stories grew up around them. Rangers themselves relieved the tedium around the camp by telling them. Some are true; some are not. The one-mob-one-Ranger story they have heard thousands of times. It will not die. Neither will the legend of the Texas Rangers.

CHAPTER II

WHAT MADE THEM

THE Texas Rangers are what they are because their enemies have been what they were. The Rangers had to be superior to their enemies to survive. Their enemies were pretty good in their way, and since the Rangers became champions, they had to be better than any that opposed them. That is the way champions are made. They do not always win, but they have to win most of the time to be champions.

Perhaps the reason they have won so many times is that their cause is a good one, something they could believe in with all their hearts. As Bill McDonald said so aptly, "It's hard to stand up agin' a man that's in the right and keeps on a comin'." The Ranger was right because he was standing between the people and their enemies, upholding the law, striking down the lawless. His was often a dangerous game but it was and is an interesting one, and the men who follow it love to play it.

The present-day force of Texas Rangers is small, and often the men have little to do. Texas is now a law-abiding place, but there were many times when it was not so. The Texas Ranger force has been large when there were a great many enemies and much law-breaking, small when peace prevailed. We might say that the Rangers have almost at times worked themselves out of a job.

Their story begins about 1823, when there was only a handful of people in Texas. At that time Texas was a part of Mexico and Mexico had belonged to Spain. It was in 1821 that a young man, Stephen F. Austin, known as the Father of Texas, made a contract to bring three hundred American families into the Spanish province of Texas. It is

[3]

doubtful if he had half that number by 1823—probably not more than six or seven hundred people. These Americans under Austin's direction settled in the southern and eastern part of the state, in the rich valleys of the Colorado, Brazos and Trinity rivers, and not far from the Gulf of Mexico. They were real pioneers in that they had left their own homes in the United States, gone into a foreign country, and settled in a perfect wilderness.

It is true that they had neighbors, but as things turned out their neighbors gave them more trouble than they had bargained for. They had Mexican neighbors along the Rio Grande, and up as far as San Antonio. For a time these Mexicans were their friends, but not for long.

The Texans' closest and most troublesome neighbors were the Indians. The Indians did not like the white men to move into their hunting grounds, run off the game and claim land which the Indians had always used as theirs. They began to strike back at the newcomers, steal their horses, burn their cabins, kill their cattle, and even murder the people.

There was no army to send after these raiders who disappeared like crows in a tall forest. Austin called the citizens together, had them organize and go in pursuit of the Indians. Because these men moved at will and went wherever they thought the Indians might be—"ranged" over the country—they were called Rangers. Austin mentioned them first in 1823, and ever after in time of danger the name of Ranger cropped up.

The Indians who lived close around the first settlers seemed bad enough, but the tribes there were small in number, not very warlike, and no match for the Texans in war. Within twenty years or less these Indians were either killed, or run out, or subdued.

Far more serious was the powerful Comanche tribe that ranged the open country to the west. Living to the west and south of the Comanches were the Apaches. These two tribes were a different breed, and there was nothing peaceful about them. As nomads, they had no permanent homes but lived in skin tepees and followed the great buffalo herds in their annual migrations. They were meat eaters, with all the ferocious character that meat eaters are supposed to develop. One thing that set them apart from the eastern Indians was their great herds of horses; they lived on horseback, played on horseback, and, what was more important to the Texans, fought on horseback. They neither gave nor asked mercy. They never surrendered, and they killed with cruel torture anyone who surrendered to them.

For fifty or sixty years, the Texas Rangers could always depend on it that the Comanches and Apaches were their enemies and that war with them was war to the death. Since these Indians were such fine horsemen, the Texans had to become horsemen, too, in order to cope with their foes. It may be said that the Indians—Comanches and Apaches chiefly—put the Texas Rangers on horseback and kept them there until the last Indian battle fought in the Devil's Mountain in far West Texas in 1881.

The other neighbors, the Mexicans in San Antonio and south to the Rio Grande, also became enemies of the Texans. It would seem from this story that the Texans were hard to get along with, and in some ways they were. Trouble with the Mexicans began within a few years after Austin brought in the first families, and the trouble grew until finally the Texans declared their independence on March 2, 1836, celebrated in the state as Texas Independence Day. They captured President Santa Anna in the battle of San Jacinto on April 21, 1836, and ended the war. Though the war was over, the fighting went on between the Texans and Mexicans as it had before. The Mexicans were also horsemen so that the Rangers found themselves under attack from two sides by mounted enemies. In order to fight on equal terms, to charge when they had an advantage and retreat when they had none, the Texas Rangers found it to their advantage to have only the best horses. They came to prize good horses highly when horses offered the fastest means for getting over the country.

It was during the Revolution that the first force of Texas Rangers was set up by law. The Texans feared if they went away to fight the Mexicans with Ben Milam, who was killed in San Antonio, or with David Crockett and Wm. B. Travis, who died in the Alamo, or with Sam Houston, who won the battle of San Jacinto, that their homes and families would be open to attack by the Indians from the west. In 1835

three companies of Rangers were created and sent to patrol the Indian border while the regular army was busy with the Mexicans. Sixty men were supposed to guard the country from the Sabine to the Colorado, a distance of several hundred miles. Fortunately, the Indians for the most part remained peaceful during the Texas Revolution, and the Rangers had little to do.

So began a three-cornered conflict for possession of Texas among three races. The Indian had his warrior, the Mexican his ranchero or cabellero, and the Texan his Ranger. All three were mounted on the best horses they could get, and all were armed with the best weapons available. They formed a triangle of conflict exciting and dramatic, and in the end the Texas Ranger emerged the champion. The memory of what he went through forms his tradition; the practices he followed have become his habit. The dress and the arms of those days explain the clothes he wears and the arms he carries today.

CHAPTER III

THE CAPTAIN COMES

AFTER Texas gained its independence of Mexico in 183ᴜ it set up a republic—the Republic of Texas—which lasted until 1846 when Texas became a state in the Union. It was during this period that the Texas Rangers became better established and began to make a name for themselves that spread far beyond the borders of the state.

Efforts were made to dispense with them, but the Comanches kept raiding from the west and the Mexicans often invaded from the south, and in such cases the Rangers were always called back into service. They were less expensive than a regular army, and they were far more effective than the local officers. Texas needed an inexpensive force of fighting men because it was poor, and it needed an effective force because it seemed always to be in danger. The Texas Rangers fit the need as a glove fits the hand.

If the Rangers became champions because they were able to win out over all opponents in the contest of battle, the officers became officers because they proved to be the best leaders among their men. In this way the Rangers differed from a regular military establishment, where men are taught to respect rank and to obey an officer whether he is any good or not. The Rangers had no military discipline, were independent by nature, and did not accept a man as leader unless he was the best in the outfit. He must have courage equal to any, judgment better than most, and physical strength to outlast his men on the longest march or the hardest ride. In time of danger, the captain never said to his men

[8]

"go," but he said to them "come," and it became part of the tradition that the officer goes first into any place of danger.

Leaders such as these could not be made. They were born, and then recognized for what they were. During the Republic several of these natural leaders showed up. Among them were such men as Ben Mc-Culloch, Sam Walker, that droll humorist Big Foot Wallace, John Mc-Mullen, and Addison Gillespie. Though these men were leaders themselves, they all respected and followed another whose name was John Coffee Hays. To Texans he was Jack, to the Indians Captain Jack, to the Mexicans he was El Diablo.

Jack Hays stands first among the first group of great Texas Rangers. He came from Tennessee, from the same part of Tennessee that furnished the nation with President Andrew Jackson and the Republic of Texas with President Sam Houston. In fact, his father named him John Coffee for one of Jackson's generals. To look at him, you would not expect him to be a leader of such tough and hardy men as the Texas Rangers. He was only five feet and ten inches tall, weighed about 160 pounds, and had such regular features that you might think him too attractive to be a real leader of fighting men. His eyes were hazel, his hair dark, and his skin almost as brown as a coffee berry. Though small in size and modest in manner, he was close built and wiry, tight wound, and seemed to be made of whipcord and whalebone. There are many stories about his endurance, and some of them may be true. He never seemed to tire, and it is said that he could run beside his galloping horse for long distances.

What set him apart and made him a famous Texas Ranger was what set every good leader of the force apart—his good judgment and intelligence. He seemed to know just where to strike and when; he seemed to know what his enemy would do before he did it. He did not have to contend with his own fear, for it was no part of him. It had been omitted in his composition.

When he first came to Texas at the age of twenty or twenty-one, he hardened his muscles as a land surveyor. This work kept him in the forest and trained him in the ways of the wilderness. He could range the wild unmarked country at will and never be lost or "turned around."

This work as a surveyor was the best training a Ranger could have in those days.

Since he grew up in Tennessee, he was a marksman when he came to Texas, and since he was surveying in Indian country, it was not long before he had an opportunity to lay aside his compass and transit for horse and gun and pursuit of Indians. In 1839 a large band of Comanches came from the plains and swept along the western edge of the settlements to the Gulf of Mexico. There they burned the town of Linnville, gathered a large herd of horses, and started north to their home on the distant prairies. Ben McCulloch, a Texas Ranger of whom we shall hear, did a Paul Revere ride to warn the settlers, who gathered and struck the Comanches at the battle of Plum Creek near Lockhart. They routed the Indians and recovered the horses. Much of the plunder was the Indian gear. Jack Hays was in this fight, but was not as prominent as McCulloch and Old Paint Caldwell, both famous Rangers.

It was shortly after this fight that Hays was made a captain and stationed at San Antonio with a small company of men. San Antonio

was an outpost of settlement, in the very edge of the Comanche country on the west and in the very edge of the Mexican country on the south. There was no place more exposed to danger than San Antonio and no better place for a Texas Ranger to gain some real experience. Hays and his men had plenty. If you can imagine a single Texan engaged in fighting a Comanche with one hand and a Mexican with the other, you will have some idea of how busy Jack Hays and his squad of Rangers were.

In 1841 he led two expeditions to Laredo, capturing the town in both cases and in the second one returning to San Antonio with several prisoners. He did this to protect the traders and to warn the raiders from Mexico that they would be paid in kind for any damage they did. The Mexicans raided, too, and not all the fault was on one side by any means.

The undeclared war between Mexico and Texas flamed along the whole border. From June, 1841, to September, 1842, Mexico sent two big expeditions into Texas, and Texas sent two big expeditions into Mexico. Hays and his Rangers had some part in three of these exciting affairs.

In June, 1841, the Texan Sante Fe expedition set out from near Austin to cross the plains and either capture or open trade with Santa Fe. Hays was busy in San Antonio and did not go along. Misfortune dogged the Sante Fe expedition. The long journey, lack of water, and Indian raids destroyed the strength of the Texans. When they reached

the vicinity of Sante Fe, they were captured by the Mexicans and sent as prisoners into the interior. A few of them were shot and the others eventually got back to Texas.

When Mexico heard of the Sante Fe expedition, it decided to strike back at Texas. General Rafel Vasquez captured San Antonio in March, 1842. He held the town two days and then withdrew toward the Rio Grande. Hays and his Rangers followed Vasquez to see what his purpose was, but were too few to attack such a large force.

MEXICO STRIKES BACK

The success of Vasquez encouraged the Mexicans to send a larger expedition to San Antonio under General Adrian Woll. Hays learned that Woll was coming, slipped up close enough to learn the size of

the force, left spies to gather information, and set out to warn the people. The Mexicans again captured the town and took many prisoners, including the court. While General Woll was in San Antonio, the Texans responded to the call of Hays, and the old fighting clan began to gather under the leadership of Matthew Caldwell and Ben McCulloch. The Texans were badly organized and outnumbered, but they began fighting as best they could as General Woll withdrew, carrying several prisoners including the members of the district court. On September 17, 1842, Old Paint Caldwell wrote from the battlefield: "The enemy are all around me on every side; but I fear them not. I will hold my position until I hear from reinforcements. Come and help me—it is the most favorable opportunity I have ever seen. There are eleven hundred of the enemy. I can whip them on my own ground without any help, but I can not take prisoners. Why don't you come?—Huzza! Huzza for Texas."

When the Texas force grew to sufficient size, Hays joined it and helped make General Woll's retreat to the Rio Grande a dangerous and risky retreat. One of the best descriptions we have of him was written by the pioneer canebrake preacher, Z. N. Morrell: "Captain Jack Hays,

our intrepid leader, five feet ten inches high, weighing one hundred sixty pounds, his black eyes flashing decision of character, from beneath a full forehead, and crowned with beautiful black hair, was soon mounted on his dark bay war-horse and on the war-path." It is said that General Woll offered five hundred dollars for Hays' head, but we cannot be sure of this. In all his long career Hays was never wounded or captured. Those who knew him said he bore a charmed life.

When Woll crossed the Rio Grande, the Texans stopped on the Texas bank and organized what is known as the Mier expedition, the second Texas expedition into Mexico. It was one thing to fight an invader; every Texan was expected to do this and most all were willing. It was something else to invade a foreign country, and only those who volunteered did so. Hays and Ben McCulloch proved their wisdom by not going to Mier, but some well-known Texas Rangers such as Samuel H. Walker and Big Foot Wallace did go, to their regret. All the Texans were captured at Mier just across the river—Mexico did not like to be invaded either. As the Texans were marched across the desert toward Mexico City, they attempted to escape, but nearly died of thirst and were recaptured by the Mexicans. Santa Anna decreed that every tenth man should be shot. The ones to be shot were chosen in an interesting manner. Into a jar was placed a bean for each man, 179 beans. There were 17 black beans and the rest were white beans. The men who drew the black beans were shot and the others were placed in prison. Sam Walker and Big Foot Wallace drew white beans. So did Ewen Cameron, but Cameron—a big Scotsman who had caused the Mexicans much trouble—was shot for extra measure. Big Foot Wallace explained how he drew a white bean. He said he noticed that the white beans were put in the jar first and the black beans last. Big Foot said "I dipped deep, and came up with a white bean." He said the only trouble he had was in getting his big hand in the jar. Big Foot Wallace made a dry joke of nearly everything, even death.

This was not the end of the Mexican trouble, however. It was not long before the whole issue flared up anew.

CHAPTER IV

TEXAS JOINS THE UNION AND THE RANGERS JOIN THE ARMY

T HE Texans who had come from the United States grew tired of trying to be a separate nation. They thought it would be a grand idea to take Texas into the Union so that they would have help in fighting either Indians or Mexicans. How helpful it would be to have the United States army to come to their aid in such unpleasant business! In 1846, the Lone Star flag was hauled down, the Stars and Stripes were raised, and the last president of the Republic, Dr. Anson Jones, stepped down to make way for the first governor, J. Pinckney Henderson. There was a new star in the flag, a new state in the Union, but the trouble was by no means over.

Mexico was furious about Texas joining the Union and sent an army to the border in protest. The United States also sent an army, and the two armies faced each other with nothing but the Rio Grande between. The fighting began in a small way; soon war was declared. The American soldiers from the old states had never fought Mexicans and did not know the country. The Texans had fought Mexicans, knew them and the country. General Zachary Taylor called for two regiments of Texas Rangers to act as scouts and spies for the American Army. Captain Jack Hays was made a colonel and given command of one regiment. Hays called the Rangers who had been with him around San Antonio and made them his captains, Ben McCulloch, Sam Walker, Big Foot Wallace and several others—all captains under Colonel Jack. Hays had five hundred Texas Rangers, more than he had ever had before, and the very best and more daring men rushed to join his outfit. It must be remembered that only a few of them had served with him before.

To look at Jack Hays' Texas Rangers you would never think they were a part of the United States Army. They had no uniform; they never drilled as other soldiers did; they never saluted their own officers, not even Colonel Jack. General Taylor liked to have them around when there was any scouting or fighting to do, but he did not care for them when they were not busy. Then they were troublesome, pretty rough on Mexicans, whom they had come to hate, and were always up to tricks which were out of line with military discipline.

Whatever their faults in peace, they were grand fellows in war. In the invasion that General Taylor made from Brownsville to Monterrey and below, the Texas Rangers always scouted the way and led the charge when the battle came. The United States army under Taylor never moved a mile that Ben McCulloch and his Rangers had not scouted in advance. McCulloch rendered more service than any Captain in the regiment, and his exploits would fill a book.

General Winfield Scott led a second invading army from Vera Cruz to Mexico City, which he captured to end the war. As soon as the fighting was over with Taylor, Hays took his Rangers to Vera Cruz, where they were used to fight guerillas in the rear of Scott's army.

On this line of march the army captured Perote Prison, where the survivors of the ill-fated expeditions of Sante Fe and Mier had been held. Many of the Rangers had been in that prison. One of them was Samuel H. Walker, now a captain. A story is told that when they reached Perote Sam Walker said that he was going to dig up the flagpole, explaining that when he was a prisoner the Mexicans made him dig the hole and set the tall pole. He put a ten-cent piece in the bottom of the hole and told his guards that he would one day return to claim his dime. The story is that Walker found his dime. He was later killed by guerillas whom he had punished severely.

Big Foot Wallace was also at Perote as a Mier Prisoner and in Mexico City. He was a giant in size and was always figuring to make his captors unhappy. They had Big Foot and other Texans building the road and made Big Foot haul a cart with road material in it. Big Foot got tired of being a horse, and so he "got scared," ran away and tore up the Mexican cart, according to legend. When he came back with the victorious army, he was still playing jokes, at least they were jokes to him. Big Foot got hungry and ordered a Mexican to bring him some bread. It occurred to him, so he said, that the Mexicans might poison the bread, and Big Foot decided to make a test. He ordered the Mexican to eat a whole loaf, and made him do it. Big Foot Wallace never married, and lived to the age of eighty-two. He is buried in the State Cemetery in Austin, and his epitaph is one of the best that could be found. It reads:

BIG FOOT WALLACE

HERE LIES HE WHO SPENT HIS

MANHOOD DEFENDING THE HOMES

OF

TEXAS

BRAVE HONEST AND FAITHFUL

BORN APRIL 3, 1817

DIED JAN. 7, 1899

His real name was William A. Wallace, but everybody called him affectionately Big Foot.

Another famous Texan with Hays was John S. Ford, who fought in the Texas Revolution, the Mexican War, and the Civil War. Ford was adjutant of Hays' Rangers, and it was his duty to make out death certificates. This duty gave him a nickname which stuck to him all his long life. When he first started making out death certificates, he would write on each one "Rest in Peace." As time went on, this was shortened to "R.I.P." The Rangers began telling each other, "Look out there, Old Rip will get you." And so John became Rip Ford.

On December 6, 1847, the Texas Rangers who landed at Vera Cruz rode into Mexico City. General Ethan Allen Hitchcock described their coming: "Hays's Rangers have come, their appearance never to be forgotten. Not in any sort of uniform, but well mounted and doubly well armed: each man has one or two Colt's revolvers besides ordinary pistols, a sword, and every man a rifle . . . they are strong athletic fellows. The Mexicans are terribly afraid of them."

Rip Ford had something to say about their entry: "Our entrance into the City of Mexico produced a sensation among the inhabitants. They thronged the streets along which we passed. The greatest curiosity prevailed to get a sight at 'Los Diabolos Tejanos'—'The Texas Devils.' "

General Hitchcock mentions that the Rangers had Colt six-shooters. The story of how they acquired and started to use Samuel Colt's gun is as thrilling as the story of their role in the Mexican War.

CHAPTER V

THE RANGER GETS HIS GUN

THE Rangers had other foes besides the Mexicans. These were the Comanches and the Apaches. The Comanches were the finest horsemen in the land and were rarely caught dismounted. Their bridle was a single thong looped around the horse's under-jaw, their saddle was no more than a piece of buffalo or deer hide to separate the sweaty man from the sweaty horse. The Indian traveled light and could cover great distances with great speed. The Comanches were splendid horse thieves, and they liked nothing better than to steal or stampede the Ranger's horses. They knew that a Ranger on foot was no Ranger at all, and in this the Ranger agreed with the Indian. He was careful of his horse. In Indian country he slept on the ground with his trusty horse nearby, hobbled or staked, and sometimes, though not often, he tied the rope that held his horse to his own wrist.

If the Ranger learned that it was dangerous to surrender to the Mexicans, he found that to surrender to a Comanche was unthinkable. The Indians had no jails, nowhere to keep a prisoner, no one to guard him. They could not be bothered with prisoners and so they killed all men prisoners, though they would often keep the women and children. The Indians did not show mercy in killing a prisoner by shooting him or killing him quickly. They liked to torture their prisoners, cause them as much pain and suffering as possible.

Sometimes the Indians would turn a prisoner over to the squaws, who would beat him. There was a red-headed Ranger named Henry Karnes, a very famous one. The Indians captured him once but for some reason did not kill him. They turned him over to the squaws, who were struck with the bright red color of his hair and of his sunburned face. He did not come up to their expectation of what a pale face ought to look like and the Indians were suspicious that he was playing some trick on them. They took Karnes to the creek, where they scrubbed him well, trying to rub off the redness. They had no luck with his hair, but they made his skin redder than it was naturally.

From both of their enemies the Texas Rangers learned some hard lessons. They learned to ride, to care for their horses, without which they felt helpless. They learned not to surrender, and rarely did.

The Rangers also learned that they were at a disadvantage, because their weapons would not permit them to fight on horseback as their enemies the Comanches did. The Indian carried a short strong bow made of Osage Orange or *bois d'arc* (meaning bow wood) and about twenty flint or steel arrows slung over his right shoulder. He could ride a horse at full speed and shoot these arrows one after another with great rapidity. He had something very close to a repeating or automatic weapon, and he could send the arrow with force enough to drive it through the body of a man. The Texans had the old-fashioned American rifle, which was accurate and of long range, but it could not be used by a man on horseback. For one thing, it was too long and too heavy. It carried only one bullet, and, since cartridges had not been invented, it required much time to load. The Ranger had to dismount to shoot with any accuracy or to reload once he had fired. The Indians knew this and they took good advantage of it. They would ride around the dismounted Rangers, rush in when the guns were empty, and retreat at will. The Rangers needed a new type of weapon, one with several shots, one that could be used on horseback.

Captain Jack Hays found just such a weapon, proved its use in Indian war, and made its inventor rich and famous all over the world. Hays and his Rangers at San Antonio saw for the first time the strange new gun that was to become most dear to them. The weapon was the revolver or six-shooter; the inventor was Samuel Colt.

Sam Colt was as inventive as Jack Hays was adventurous. Though one lived in Connecticut and the other far away in Texas, and though they probably never met, they were strangely related in the strange enterprise of finding and proving a weapon that a mounted man could use on equal or superior terms with the Comanche or any other horseman.

Colt invented a revolver before Jack Hays came to Texas, and a factory began making them. The only trouble was that Colt could not sell his new-fangled pistol in the United States. The army found fault with it and refused to buy it, and no one else bought it either. The Colt factory at Paterson, New Jersey, went out of business in the year that Hays declined to cross the Rio Grande with the ill-fated Mier expedition, in 1842. It is not certain Hays had the revolver at that time, though we know that some of the Colt guns were in Texas by 1839, and Hays must have seen them.

What we do know is that while Hays was in and near San Antonio some of the Colt revolvers were sent to his camp. They must have created a lot of excitement because fighting men are always interested in weapons, and they want only the best. Here was a new weapon, one that would carry six shots, one that could be used by a man on horseback. We can imagine how these young Rangers talked about the shiny new six-shooters, took them apart, put them together, and wondered if they would really work. The only way to find out was to try them.

A target was chosen, probably a tree about as thick as a man, and some Ranger, maybe Hays himself, made the test. It was a great success. In less than one minute, one man placed six leaden balls in one target. Then a Ranger mounted a trusty horse and tried the gun out with the horse in motion. The aim was not as good, but it was clear that a Ranger on a running horse could shoot a running Comanche if he could get close enough. That night there must have been much excitement and little sleep as the Rangers talked of trying the six-shooters out on the Comanches in the very next fight.

They did not have long to wait, for the Comanches were coming in close to the settlements. The fight took place on the Pedernales River north and west of San Antonio. Hays told his men to dismount as they usually did, and when the Indians came in range on their running horses, to fire at them with their long-range rifles, then to mount their own horses and go in pursuit, using the Colt revolvers. He told them also to get as close as they could to the Indians so they could hit the target when they shot. He said to powder-burn them.

When the Indians made the attack, they had the surprise of their lives. They found the Rangers in hot pursuit with guns popping, more guns than the Indians had ever heard before. The chief escaped, and remarked that he never wanted to meet Jack Hays and his Rangers again. He wanted no part of men who had a shot for every finger on

one hand. The Rangers had at last found the ideal weapon, one suited to their need. Now they could meet the Indians on horseback. When Colt found that his first model gun was being used by the Rangers, he named it the "Texas." But the Texans could not buy enough guns to keep Colt from going broke. Whether he went broke and closed his factory before or after the Rangers found a use for his weapon, we do not know. We know that this first gun was imperfect, and it was only when Jack Hays formed his regiment in the United States Army that the Colt revolver had a real chance to prove its worth.

Here is how Hays put Colt back into business:

When Hays formed his regiment in 1846, the handful of men with him in San Antonio had Colt revolvers and knew how to use them. They became his officers and carried their trusty guns into service. The other men—probably 475 out of the 500—had the old style single-shot pistols, or maybe only a rifle. Every man wanted a gun as good as those carried by Hays, McCulloch, and Walker. They wanted six-shooters and not single-shooters. They wanted pistols as well as rifles. They did not hesitate to make their wants known, for Rangers are plain-speaking men. Hays agreed with them, and sent an order to Washington for 1000 Colt revolvers so that each Ranger could have two.

Sam Colt had not made a revolver in five years, and the government had to hunt him up in New England, where he had set up as a medicine

showman. He had no model of the guns he had once manufactured, and had to design a new one. It seems that Sam Walker met Colt in New York to talk with him about changes the Rangers wanted made in the new revolvers. Colt adopted Walker's suggestions and named this second gun the "Walker." He delivered the thousand big six-shooters to Hays before the Rangers left Vera Cruz.

There in Mexico the whole United States Army, which included Robert E. Lee, U. S. Grant, Jefferson Davis, George B. McClellan, and scores of other men who became generals, saw these terrible Texans and what they could do with their weapons. The Army now wanted six-shooters; the whole world wanted revolvers. Colt reaped the benefit and died rich. Colt had helped the Texas Rangers by making a gun they could use on horseback. The Texas Rangers helped Colt by proving the gun and introducing it in war to the whole world.

CHAPTER VI

RIP FORD AND IRON JACKET

B IG events were afoot in Texas and in the United States after the Mexican War. In the eyes of Texans it would have been wise to keep Jack Hays' Texas Rangers and let them keep the peace on both the Mexican and Indian borders, but the United States had to consider the regular army and give it something to do. It could not afford to let such a band of undisciplined and ununiformed men take over a job that the army was supposed to handle. In the eyes of regular army men, the Rangers were a little too rough with the enemy. So all the experienced Rangers were dismissed from the service.

About the time they were set free, gold was discovered in California and many of the Rangers joined the rush to the diggings. Hays went to California, where he became sheriff and made a fortune in land. As far as we know, he never returned to Texas. Ben McCulloch and John McMullen went, but McCulloch was soon back in Texas. Rip Ford remained in Texas and may be considered the leader of the Rangers during the dozen years separating the Mexican and Civil wars.

The Texas Rangers were called back into service because the regular army did not do what the Texans expected. The Texans expected too much. They wanted the army to kill every Indian that entered the settlements, drive the others out of the state, and kill every Mexican that was caught on the Texas side of the Rio Grande with a gun in his hand. The army was under strict orders to protect the Indians, who were wards of Uncle Sam, and it was under severe regulations in dealing with a foreign country and its citizens in peacetime. Both the Indians and the Mexicans knew of this mild policy and they frequently took advantage of it. They did not fear the regular soldier as they did the Texas Rangers. It was the old story of calling in the Rangers to do what the people wanted and what nobody else would or could do. The army wouldn't do the job, the citizens couldn't, and so the Rangers did.

For ten years—1848 to 1858—the Rangers were in and out of service. They bickered with the Indian agents, grumbled about the regular soldiers, chased fugitive Indian bands, sat in Indian councils, and occasionally had a brush with the Mexicans. In 1858 Governor Hardin R. Runnels came into office with war in his eye, determined to protect the frontier with Texas Rangers and pay them with Texas funds. He appointed John S. Ford in supreme command, and gave Old Rip the title of Senior Captain. War flamed again from the Rio Grande to the Red River, and 1848–1860 may be known as the bloody years.

When Ford left Austin for the Comanche frontier in February, 1858, he had orders from the governor which read: "I impress on you the necessity of action and energy. Follow any and all trails of hostile or suspected hostile Indians you may discover, and, if possible, overtake and chastise them, if unfriendly." The governor did not say take prisoners. What he really said was to kill the Indians if you can. The Rangers liked such simple orders.

By March 19, Ford had reached the Indian reservation on the Clear Fork of the Brazos in what is now Young County where he picked up a hundred friendly Indians under Captain Shapley P. Ross to act as spies in the Comanche hunt. If you had been in north Texas on April 22, 1858, you could have seen what a Ranger expedition looked like. Ford had 102 men, two wagons, an ambulance, and fifteen pack mules, while Captain Ross had 113 friendly Indians from the reservation nearby. A week later Ford crossed the Red River into what is now Oklahoma, something he had no right to do. On May 10, the spies killed a buffalo and found in it two Comanche arrowheads, and on the following day they saw some Comanches. The Rangers and their Indian allies attacked the Comanche camp early on the morning of May 12, when spring was breaking all over the land. Ford said that he had fought three hundred warriors, that his men killed seventy-six Indians, cap-

[27]

tured over three hundred horses, took eighteen prisoners, mostly women and children, and lost two killed and two wounded.

Among the Indians killed was the chief Iron Jacket. He got his name because he wore a coat of mail, said to have come down from the Spaniards. Iron Jacket was supposed to be bullet-proof, and he must have thought so, for he appeared in full dress, trusting to his iron shingles. The Rangers concentrated their fire on him, killed his horse, and riddled him with bullets.

As we look back on this fight, it does not appear to be important. Ford thought it was important. He said it proved that the Indians could be followed into their own country and defeated on their own ground. What it did show was the Texas Rangers were acting in the old tradition by finding the enemy and hitting him hard without much regard for ordinary law or the rules of war. The Indians were being destroyed, and this fight was but one part of that destruction which would have gone on anyway.

CHAPTER VII

NORTH GOES THE INDIAN

I F YOU look at a map of the United States, and especially the western half, you will find a large number of Indian Reservations. They are in New Mexico, Arizona, the Dakotas, Montana, Wyoming, and many other states. The biggest reservation of all—the Indian state—is now Oklahoma, known for a long time as Indian Territory.

Look as you may, you will find no United States Indian reservation in Texas, probably the only western state that does not have one. And for this absence of Indians in the Lone Star State, the Texans are responsible. We have seen that the Rangers were used to drive the Indians north of Red River and that they pursued them even into their own Indian Territory.

It was not the fault of the United States that Texas does not have to-day some Red Men to give interest and variety to its population. Uncle Sam did set up two reservations in what are now Young and Throckmorton counties. One, known as the Brazos Reservation, was on the Brazos River, and on it was gathered the small and friendly tribes, such as the Caddo, Anadarko, Waco, and Tonkawa. Approximately two thousand of these Indians lived on this reservation from about 1855 to 1859. These were the Indians that went with Rip Ford under Captain L. S. Ross when he defeated the Comanches north of Red River in 1858.

Near the Brazos Reserve, in present Throckmorton County, was another Indian Reservation for the Comanches. The number was small,

[30]

because the Comanches were wild and warlike and did not care for life on a Reservation.

Major Robert S. Neighbors was appointed Indian agent on the Reservation. He represented the United States government, not Texas, and he did everything he could to make the experiment a success. His main job was trying to protect the Indians from the Texans.

There was always trouble around the Reservation. The Indians lived by hunting, and they would slip away with or without permission to find game. The settlers were afraid of the Indians, and to them all Indians looked alike. When they saw one, they were likely to shoot him before they inquired whether he was on the warpath or a buffalo hunt. The wild Comanches in the Indian Territory and farther west hated the Reservation Indians, killed them when they could, or made raids, knowing that the blame would be laid on the Reserve Indians.

It would be a tribute to the Texas Rangers if we could say that they were sent to this trouble spot and that they were able to restore order. This could not be done because the Reservation was under the control of the United States, and the Rangers had no business meddling there.

The United States soldiers could protect the Indians *on* the Reservation, which was only a few thousand acres, but they could not give protection *off* the Reservation. The soldier had no more right to shoot or capture a Texan off the Reserve than the Rangers had to shoot or capture an Indian on it. Indians continued to depredate, and Texans continued to kill them. The situation became intolerable to both sides. The Texans demanded that all Indians should be driven from Texas, and in 1859 the United States government ordered Major Neighbors to lead all Reserve Indians north of Red River and find a place for them in the Indian Territory.

Ford was present for at least a part of the time around the Reserves, but he did not act with the directness that was his custom. Then came

another Texas Ranger, John Henry Brown, but he gave Major Neighbors little help. The Indians could not gather their stock because the Texas Rangers would not let them leave the Reserve without an escort, and Major Neighbors would not consent to having them escorted by

Texans. The Indians had to abandon their stock. They had to leave before any home had been provided for them in the Indian Territory.

INTO THE INDIAN TERRITORY

It was in the hot days of August, 1859, that a strange cavalcade pointed north from the Texas Reserves. There were several wagons loaded with Indian gear and such personal belongings as the fugitives might have collected in Texas. Most of the Indians walked or rode on horses. Ahead of them, behind them, and on their flanks rode the United States cavalry. Somewhere with them, in civilian clothes, was their stern, honest, and devoted agent, Robert S. Neighbors. On August

8, he crossed Red River, leaving Texas with its bitter people behind, but nobody in Texas felt more bitter than did Major Neighbors.

That night, safe at last in the Indian Territory, he sat in camp with

his Indians around him and wrote the last letter that his wife was to get from him. It may have been the last letter he ever wrote. He said:

I have this day crossed all the Indians out of the heathen land of Texas and am now out of the land of the Philistines.

If you want . . . a full description of our Exodus out of Texas—Read the "Bible" where the children of Israel crossed the Red Sea. We have had about the same show, only our enemies did not follow us to Red River. If they had— the Indains would have in all probability sent them back without the interposition of Divine providence.

The bad luck of the Indians was not over. Major Neighbors had no place for them, so he moved them in with the Wichitas in the Washita valley. Here their old enemies, the Comanches, found them a few months later and destroyed them completely.

Major Neighbors, having completed his mission as best he could, returned to Texas, passing through Fort Belknap, which was near the now vacated Indian Reserve. He was riding south to San Antonio for a visit with his family, from whom he had been long separated.

What Major Neighbors forgot for the moment was the enemies he had made in Texas as a protector of the Indians. Now the struggle was over, bygones would be bygones. Since he was such a decent person, he might have felt this way as he stood talking in Fort Belknap with a friend. Then Edward Cornett, whom Neighbors probably did not know, shot and killed him without warning. They buried him at Belknap near the place where he had tried so hard to preserve a safe home for Indians in Texas.

I once knew an ex-Ranger who claimed that he was with a company near Fort Belknap when Major Neighbors was killed. He said that the Texas Rangers went after Cornett, caught him, and gave him justice without judge or jury.

With the removal of the Reserve Indians, we come to the end of an era. There are now no Indians, save a handful on a small reserve in Polk County in East Texas, who could live legally in Texas. They were all looked on as invaders, to be driven out or killed if they came. For thirty years, they made raids, from the Indian Territory, from New Mexico, and from the Rio Grande, but in every case the Texas Rangers met them if they could and dealt as harshly as the Texans desired.

CHAPTER VIII

RED BEARD OF THE SOUTH BORDER

WHILE the Rangers were fighting the Indians around the Red River, trouble with the Mexicans was brewing six hundred miles away along the Rio Grande. The place where it started was Brownsville at the southernmost tip of Texas. The one who started it had a red beard as well as a stout heart.

One of the oldest Spanish families in that land was named Cortinas, and in this family was a son named Juan Nepomuceno. At the time Juan Cortinas started on the road to fame as a defender of the Mexicans he was twenty-five years old. His family was wealthy and proud, but probably not very proud of Juan, who was a rough and rowdy *vaquero*. He would not go to school and did not learn to write until he became governor of Tamaulipas. He was a horseman and a fighter, and his enemy, Adolphus Glavecke, charged him with murder, robbery and horse theft, but Juan was never convicted.

The Mexicans called him "Cheno." He was of medium size, his hair was brown, eyes green or gray; and his beard red. He was a natural leader and did not know the meaning of fear.

Every morning it was Cheno's custom to ride in from the rancho for a cup of coffee and some conversation at the tavern in Brownsville. He was already popular, but what he did on the morning of July 13, 1859, made him a hero in the eyes of the Mexicans and a villain in the eyes of the Texans, a role he was to play to the end of his long life.

In the place where Cheno drank coffee was one of the Cortinas' family servants, who had had too much to drink. The city marshal—the

Texans had taken over all the offices—named Robert Shears arrested the drunken Mexican and began to abuse and mistreat him.

Cheno Cortinas made a mild protest at the unnecessary brutality, and Shears replied with an insult. Cheno promptly shot Shears, rescued the servant, put him on his horse behind him, and galloped away to his ranch. This act infuriated the Texans and delighted the Mexicans, who were fed up with the newcomers anyway.

The Texans prepared to hunt Cheno but never got around to it. Word came that Cortinas was gathering men and horses, some in Mexico, some in Texas. September 28—fourteen days after Major Neighbors had been killed—Cheno struck Brownsville like a tornado. He had chosen well, for many of the Texans had gone across the river to a ball in Matamoros. They were late in returning and came in with much noise and merrymaking. There was so much noise that when Cortinas' guns were heard the sleepy people's only thought was that the party in Matamoros must have been a great success.

Through the din came the pounding hoofs of a hundred horses and the sound of yelling and shots. Those who were awake finally made out *"Viva* Cheno Cortinas! *Mueran los Gringos! Viva la Republica de México!"* Hurrah for Cheno Cortinas! Death to the Gringos! Hurrah for Mexico! Strange sounds indeed.

By daylight Cortinas had captured the town, killed three Americans, and intended to kill Glavecke, his chief enemy, and Shears, whom he called "the squinting sheriff." He broke open the jail, freed all the prisoners, and killed the jailer. He even captured the United States military post, Fort Brown, which had just been vacated because the troops had been sent to help Major Neighbors move the Reserve Indians. He tried to run up the Mexican flag on the American flagpole but failed for lack of tackle. The Texans were helpless before the forces of Cortinas, and they sent out cries for help in all directions. They were afraid to go on the street or to gather in groups. They laid low while Cheno hunted for his enemies.

Across the river Cheno's cousin, Miguel Tijerina, commanded some Mexican cavalry. He and another Mexican army officer came over and persuaded Cortinas to withdraw from Brownsville. Cheno moved to his mother's ranch and issued a call to all downtrodden Mexicans to join him. He said, "Our . . . enemies shall not possess our lands until they have fattened it with their own gore."

If there ever was a time when a company of good Texas Rangers was needed it was during the weeks following. Cortinas did not come to Brownsville, but he defeated every body of citizens who went to find him. One group of fighting men called themselves the Brownsville Tigers. The Tigers were made up of a mixture of Mexicans and Americans, and they were going to bring Cortinas in—dead or alive. The Mexican Tigers borrowed a cannon from Mexico, and the Americans took one from Fort Brown. There was no doubt great competition to see who would win the honors. The brave army marched out of Brownsville on October 22, and found Cortinas. There was some fighting, but not much. There was great competition between the Mexican Tigers and the Texas Tigers to see which Tiger would get to Brownsville first. The Texans won, making it in forty minutes, according to one report. Both sets of Tigers traveled light, leaving their cannon in the hands of Cortinas. This fight at Santa Rita was on October 24, 1859.

Cheno's force grew larger as news of his victory spread. Each morning at six o'clock, what was left of the Brownsville Tigers were shamed to hear through the river fog the cannon booming salutes from the camp of Cortinas. His green-gray eyes danced as he recalled the flight of the

[37]

Tigers. He let it be known that he did not return to Brownsville because he had many friends there and he did not want them harmed. He only wanted the squinting sheriff and one or two other enemies.

Shortly after the Tiger fight, a Captain W. G. Tobin arrived at Brownsville with a company of so-called Rangers. They were not experienced, not worthy to be called Rangers. It has been said that Tobin had one good man in his outfit, but he fell off a gun carriage and broke his neck shortly after reaching the place. They took one of Cortinas' friends from the jail and hanged him before they set out after the main actor. On Palo Alto Prairie—scene of many clashes—Cortinas met them, killed three Rangers, and drove the others back to Brownsville.

Tobin now marched on Santa Rita, where the Tigers had had such bad luck. Like them, he carried a cannon. Again Cortinas won, but the routed Rangers managed to save their cannon, which may have been lighter than the ones the Tigers lost. This second fight was on November 25, 1859.

On December 5, Major Heintzelman wrote Col. Robert E. Lee from Brownsville:

> Cortinas was now a great man; he had defeated the "Gringos," and his position was impregnable; he had the Mexican flag flying in his camp, and numbers were flocking to his standard. When he visited Matomoros he was received as the champion of his race—as a man who would right the wrongs the Mexicans had received; that would drive the hated Americans to the Nueces.

With 165 soldiers and 120 of Tobin's Rangers, Major Heintzelman left Brownsville on December 14 for Cortinas' camp. They came in sight of a barricade of ebony logs. Major Heintzelman ordered Tobin's men to spy out the camp and see what was behind the barricade, but Tobin's Rangers had been made skittish by their last experience when they stampeded, and it was all the Major could do to keep them from stampeding again.

There was nothing behind the ebony barricade, for Cortinas had withdrawn a week before. The force advanced three miles and found him. Cortinas opened fire on United States troops, and this was the beginning of his downfall. The Americans captured the camp, killing eight Mexicans. Two regulars were wounded and one of Tobin's Rangers was killed, but Cortinas rode into the brush unharmed.

RIP FORD INTO THE FIGHT

Rip Ford and fifty-three Rangers heard the guns of the fight at La Ebronal but were too late to get in the scrap. They had been on the road from Austin for a month. In November, Ford, just back from the Indian Reservation, was ordered to Brownsville by Governor Runnels. All sorts of rumors were flying about what Cortinas was doing to the southern border, and Ford was urged to hurry. Had you been in Austin in that November, you might have seen Old Rip Ford ride down Congress Avenue, ferry across the Colorado River and head south to Brownsville nearly five hundred miles away. His squad of Rangers numbered eight men, armed with pistols and rifles, but Ford picked up recruits on the way and got to Brownsville with a company of fifty-seven men. These Rangers created a sensation when they rode into Brownsville on December 14, and the home guards thought for a time that Cortinas was on them again. Ford's Rangers were much better than Tobin's, for Ford knew what a Ranger ought to be and would have only good men.

Cheno's days of victory were now past. The United States troops and the Texas Rangers under Ford moved up the river, and Cortinas retreated before them until he reached Rio Grande City, which was no city at all but a hamlet lying between the hills on the north and the Rio Grande on the south. Here he made his stand and here the combined force of soldiers and Rangers struck him on December 26 while the Christmas candles were burning. The Mexicans could not stand before the superior force, and so they stampeded and all that could "jumped the river" into Mexico. Cortinas again escaped without a scratch.

There was still some fighting, a little in Texas, a little in Mexico, but the Cortinas war was virtually over after the fight at Rio Grande City. Cortinas later became a general in the Mexican army and a governor of his own state. Throughout his long career he did not care for Texans, and for this we can not blame him. He was causing Texans trouble twenty-five years later when he was an important man, but he was careful to stay on the Mexican side of the river.

CHAPTER IX

BANDITS ON THE RIO GRANDE

AFTER Rip Ford helped the United States troops put Cortinas out of Texas at Rio Grande City, in 1860, the Rangers had little importance. They were dwarfed by four years of Civil War, ten more years when the South was occupied by northern troops in so-called Reconstruction. These were bitter years in which the Texans had little control over their own business and Texas Rangers were not permitted.

It was in 1874 that the Texans regained control and elected Richard Coke governor. One of the first acts of Governor Coke was to reorganize the Rangers.

There had never been greater need for them. On the west the Indians had driven back the settlers, and on the Rio Grande Cortinas was still sending his raiders to steal cattle. There was a third trouble which the Rangers had not dealt with before. Lawless men—singly and in bands —had risen to terrorize the people within the state. The Rangers had to fight Indians on the West, Mexicans on the South, and outlaws among the people. The Rangers rose to the need, and this was in many respects their finest period of service.

The two men that Governor Coke sent for were L. H. McNelly and John B. Jones. Both men had been officers in the Confederate army and had experience which prepared them well for the work they had to do.

Captain L. H. McNelly was a small frail man with deep blue eyes and brown hair over a high forehead and a thin face. He wore a mustache and beard, as most men did in those days. His voice was soft and gentle. There was nothing about his delicate body or his voice or manner to indicate the iron will that he carried in this frail form.

He was placed in command of a Special Force of Texas Rangers intended for use in southwest Texas and along the Mexican border. McNelly was thirty years old, but he was already a seasoned warrior. He entered the Confederate army at the age of seventeen and became a captain at nineteen; he was given the dangerous duty of scouting and making forays inside the enemy lines. He knew horses and men and what they could do, but of fear he knew nothing. He was especially skilled in using spies, and he always had one or more in the ranks of the enemy to tell him what the plans of the enemy were.

McNelly's first assignment was to deal with the bad men who had shown up in Texas, men who were terrorizing their own people, taking the law into their own hands. He went first to Cuero in DeWitt County, where the Sutton-Taylor feud had broken out. He brought some measure of peace to this strife-torn community before he moved south to the Rio Grande, where there was much to do.

On April 18, 1875, the following telegram came to Austin.

IS CAPT MCNELLY COMING? WE ARE IN TROUBLE, FIVE RANCHES BURNED BY DISGUISED MEN NEAR LAPARRA LAST WEEK. ANSWER.

JOHN MCCLURE.

Captain McNelly went to LaParra and reported that armed bands were ranging in the country, that the Mexicans and the Americans were at war murdering men and burning property. "I immediately issued an order . . . disbanding all . . . armed bands acting without the authority of the state; my order was obeyed, or agreed to be. Had I not disbanded these companies . . . it is possible that civil war would have ensued, as the Mexicans are very much exasperated."

From this scene McNelly moved on to Brownsville, where there was much cattle-stealing from across the river. Our red-bearded friend Cortinas had become a powerful man in Mexico. He had a contract to furnish beef to the Cuban government, had established himself at Bagdad near the mouth of the Rio Grande, and was reducing his expenses by sending raiding parties into Texas to steal cattle and horses. Half of his men were riding horses with American brands, and he was loading a steamer with four hundred head of cattle, two thirds of which came from the Texas side. There were one-hundred-fifty soldiers at Fort Brown, but they were inexperienced Negroes and no match for Cortinas' raiders. McNelly reported all this, and closed his letter to General Wm. Steele by saying, "I think you will hear from me soon."

The events which followed took place between June 5 and 12, 1875. One of Captain McNelly's men has told the story of how the Rangers dealt with Mexican bandits caught driving a herd of Texas cattle towards the Rio Grande. They were Cortinas' best bravos, well-mounted and well-armed. The story of the Red Raid is in Bill Callicott's own words.

BILL CALLICOTT'S STORY

"In the early spring of 1875 Captain McNelly had orders to organize a company of Rangers to go to the Rio Grande to deal with the Mexican cow thieves and bandits that were killing people and driving cattle into Mexico. Captain McNelly had orders to kill those caught on this side of the river and to take no prisoners. . . .

"We had not been out there but a little while when we heard of a band

[43]

of Mexicans who had come over after cattle. Only thirty men were in camp, the rest being out on scout. Captain McNelly called for twenty-two volunteers. Among them was Berry Smith, the youngest fellow in the company. Old Man Smith, who was with us, went to the Captain and asked him to let some other boy take Berry's place, said that Berry was the only child and if anything happened to him his mother would die of grief.

"The Captain agreed, but Berry would not have it. He said, 'Captain, we have been out here some time and haven't had a fight yet. If I get killed, it will be no worse than for some of the other boys to get killed.' I will tell you later how Berry got killed.

"Another Ranger we had with us was Old Casuse Sandaval (Jesus Sandaval). He was a Mexican who once had a ranch on this side of the river. Several years before we went out there, he and an American caught four Mexican cow thieves and hung them all to one tree. The Mexicans swore they would kill him on the first chance. Casuse had not slept in his own house for over ten years because he was afraid of being killed. He knew the country well, knew the Mexicans for miles around, and the Captain let him join the Rangers. He gave Casuse a Colt's 45 and a needle gun. Casuse was proud of these weapons and made a fine Ranger. The way he helped us in handling spies will be told later.

"We did not use pack-mules, but tied what little grub we had . . . to our saddles and started out to find the bandits. In a day or two (June 8) we caught the first Mexican bandit spy. We handled spies in this way. Old Casuse would talk to the Mexican a little, and if he was a citizen of Texas, we let him go at once. But if he was a bandit one of us would take charge of him until we saw a suitable tree. Old Casuse would put a rope around the bandit's neck, throw the end over a limb, pull him up and let him down until he would tell all he knew.

"After the Captain had all the information he would let Casuse have charge of the spy. Casuse would make a hangman's knot, place the loop over the bandit's head, throw the rope over a limb, make the bandit get on Casuse's old paint horse, and stand up in the saddle. Casuse would then make the rope fast, hit the horse a hard lick and the horse would jump from under the spy, breaking his neck instantly. We caught several spies on that scout and dealt with them all alike.

[44]

"The last spy we caught the Captain turned over to me to guard. He rode along with me until we stopped to get supper on a little creek. I had him tied with a rope so he could not get away. I fixed a little supper for him and gave him all the jerked beef and bread that he could eat and good strong coffee, knowing that would be about his last meal. I gave him some cigarettes to smoke. He enjoyed it all.

"All had had supper, and our horses had grazed for two hours. The sun was getting low when the Captain, Tom Sullivan (the Interpreter), and two of the boys came over to where I was sitting down with the bandit smoking.

" 'Bill, did you give him plenty to eat?' asked the Captain.

" 'Yes,' I said, 'all he can digest on six feet of rope.'

" 'Well,' said the Captain, 'we will relieve you; we will take charge of the prisoner.'

"They took him out to a little motte. Casuse took his old paint horse that he used for a trap-door gallows and I knew it was checking-up time for the Mexican bandit spy. They did not stay out there but a little while when the Captain and all the boys came to camp, all except Casuse and the bandit. Finally, Casuse got in and he said: 'He all right —he come back no more.' It was sundown. The next day we would go after the bandits who were driving the cattle."

If you feel that the treatment of the spy was harsh, you must remember that the times were hard. McNelly was dealing with dangerous men. He had a small force, could not guard prisoners, could not turn them loose to spread alarm. And so he killed them. His was a rough way, but it was effective and made border thieves have great respect for the slender, blue-eyed, soft-spoken Captain who had come to restore order.

CHAPTER X

DEAD MEN ON PALO ALTO PRAIRIE

W E NOW prepared to go after the bandits," continued Bill Callicott. "The spy had told us that seventeen Mexicans and one American were driving two hundred and fifty head of cattle towards Palo Alto Prairie. He told the truth. We planned to overhaul them in the night.

"I had on the only white shirt in the crowd. The Captain came to me and said:

" 'Bill, from what the spy says we will be likely to overhaul the bandits in the night and it will be hard to tell our men from them if we get mixed up. I want your white shirt, but I will give you another.'

"He tore up my white shirt and tied a piece around the left arm of each man. Berry Smith, the boy who was killed the next day, still had the piece of white tied to his arm. I went in my undershirt.

"After all was ready Captain ordered us into line and told us what to do when we hit the bandits. He told us to form a straight line, with some distance between, not to break the line and get in each other's way, or get mixed up with the bandits.

" 'Don't pay any attention to the cattle,' he said. 'We're after bandits. If they stampede, pick you out the one nearest you, keep him in front of you and keep after him. Get as close to him as you can before you shoot. It makes no difference in what direction he goes, stay with him to the finish. These are Cortinas's picked men, and he says they can cope with any Rangers or regulars. But if we can overhaul them in open country, we will teach them a lesson they will never forget.

" 'That is all I have to say. Ready! Form in twos! March!'

"Old Casuse took the lead and we rode all night. We got to Palo Alto Prairie about sunup. We found the bandit trail leading across it towards the Rio Grande. We followed it at a fast trot and lope, not wanting to overspeed our horses that had been under saddle for twenty-four hours with little rest and little to eat.

"We hadn't followed the trail more than a mile or two when we came in sight of them. The Captain knew we had the bandits right where he wanted them, and he kept getting faster and faster. The bandits saw us but thought we were regular soldiers and that they could stand us off. So the one that got away told after he got back to Mexico.

"The bandits came to a big lagoon running out from the bay in the Gulf. The lagoon was about one-hundred-fifty yards wide with mud and water from knee deep to belly deep to our horses. Captain McNelly ordered us to form a line about four feet apart, not to fire a shot until

we got on hard ground. The bandits opened fire on us from behind their horses. Their bullets would pass over our heads, between us, or hit the mud and water before us. By the time we got out of the deepest mud and water, the Mexicans mounted and away they went. Captain McNelly sent some Rangers to cut them off, and they stopped and opened fire on us. Two of them were soon killed, and the rest broke out full tilt across Palo Alto Prairie with the Rangers behind them and on the side. We were running in line, had the bandits straight ahead of us going toward the Rio Grande.

" 'When we came in gun range,' Lieutenant Robinson shouted: 'Go for them, boys! Go for them.'

"Every man slapped spurs to his horse, giving him all the speed he had. I was riding Old Ball. I rammed both spurs to him. He opened up his throttle with an unexpected lunge, went from under my hat and came near going from under me.

"We soon got up with them and the battle opened right. As fast as we overhauled one, we would shoot him or his horse. The last one we killed was riding the best horse in the bandit crowd and kept ahead of the rest. The Captain and three or four of us were after him. We killed his horse from under him near a little Spanish dagger thicket and he ran into the thicket on foot.

"We surrounded the thicket, Captain McNelly got off his horse, drew his pistol and went in on foot. He met the bandit and they were about six or eight feet apart. The bandit had emptied his pistol and the Captain had only one ball left in his. The Mexican drew his Bowie knife, started to Captain McNelly, saying: 'Me gotta you now.' The Captain leveled his pistol and placed the last shot he had between the bandit's teeth. We dismounted and ran in to find the Captain standing over the bandit who had already checked up and breathed his last.

"Captain McNelly took his knife and pistol. I untied his sash, tying it around myself. It was the prettiest I have ever seen, having the colors of Mexico—red, white and green.

"Having put an end to the last bandit, we mounted our horses and started back over the trail of the dead. It was about two o'clock in the evening. I had no hat, because Old Ball had jumped out from under it at the beginning of the fight. I happened to come upon a dead bandit laying in the grass with his hands and legs lying out straight from his body. He was shot through the head and I don't think he ever moved a muscle after he fell from his horse. His eyes were glared wide open, gazing at the hot June sun. His shaggy black beard was bloodstained, and flies were swarming over his face after blood and brains. Just back of his head, in the grass, lay a fine Mexican hat, bottom up. The high June sun was getting mighty hot to my head. So I eased down off Old Ball, picked up the hat, pulled up some grass, wiped off what blood I could, and put it on. Glad to get it. Then I got on Old Ball and overtook the Captain and the boys.

" 'Where did you get your Mexican hat?' asked the Captain. I told him I got it off a dead bandit.

" 'It is a good one,' he said. 'With that hat and sash you could pass for a Mexican bandit in the dark anywhere.'

"Old Casuse and two Mexican ranchmen began to gather up the dead bandits. When they found one, they would fasten a rope around his neck and drag him in by the saddle horn. They put them all in one pile.

"Near the end of the trail we found Spencer Adams on his horse, Sorrel Top, watching a pond. Spencer had pulled off his shirt and wrapped it around Sorrel Top's neck to protect a bullet wound from flies.

" 'What are you watching in that pond, Adams?' asked the Captain.

" 'I am watching that bandit,' said Adams.

" 'How come he's there?' inquired the Captain.

" 'This morning when the fight started by the lagoon you all got ahead of me and Berry Smith. Some of you shot the bandit off his horse and thought he was dead. Berry and I saw him crawl into that Spanish dagger thicket near the edge of this pond. We ran up to the thicket to shoot him again, but just as we got there he shot and killed Berry Smith, and shot at me and hit Sorrel Top in the neck. He got Berry's pistol and a little while ago he crawled out to this pond of water. He is about the middle of it—you can see the rush grass move when he crawls along. I think you broke his leg for he has not been on his feet today.'

"We fired several shots without waking him up. Finally one of the boys hit him. He floundered and kicked, and sometimes his feet would go over the rush grass. When he quieted down, the Captain said:

" 'Ride in, Casuse, and bring him out.' Casuse took him to the other bandits. We had killed all but one, including the American. When Casuse got back after taking the pond bandit in, we were all together except Berry Smith. We found him lying within four feet of the thicket stiff dead. He was only sixteen years old, had had no experience, and got too close to the bandit without seeing him.

" 'Bill,' the Captain said to me, 'do you know how to tie a dead man on a horse?'

" 'Yes, sir.' He told me to tie Berry Smith on Old Ball, and when it was done he looked at the work and said it was a good job. 'Bill, you must have done it before,' he said. I told him it was the first dead man, but I had tied all other kinds of packs on mules when I was with Major Jones on the northern frontier.

"We captured only two horses, one a big paint and the other a little bay. We named the paint Jack Ellis for the American we killed, and the little bay we called Cortinas. We killed the horses that were badly

[51]

wounded so they would not suffer and gathered all the Mexican saddles and bridles.

"We were now ready to march. The Captain told me to ride Berry Smith's horse and lead Old Ball with the dead Ranger tied on. We were going to Brownsville to turn our Ranger boy over to the undertaker. I marched in the rear.

"We camped on a creek where there was water and good grass for our horses. The Captain got us a little bread and beef from a ranch. Between sundown and dark the Captain came around where I was lying down resting. He told me I was on first picket duty. I saddled Old Ball and told him I was ready. The Captain said to me:

" 'You haven't had any sleep for twenty-four hours. Do you think you can stand it without going to sleep?'

" 'Yes,' I said.

" 'I guess you know the penalty where a picket goes to sleep on duty. It is death. Come on. I will locate you.'

"If Casuse had been along on his paint horse I would have thought they were taking me out to hang me as they had the bandit spy. To tell the truth, I looked like one with one dead bandit's hat on my head and another's sash around my waist.

"We went about a half mile to a thicket near the forks of two roads coming from the river.

" 'Now you keep a close lookout,' the Captain said, 'and if you see anybody coming, ride out and halt them, and if they don't stop, fire into them and come back to camp as fast as you can. You will have to stand here four hours if you don't get killed before your time is up.'

"He left me alone with the dead bandit's hat and sash. It was so dark I could hardly see my hand before my eyes. I had been raised near my old home graveyard which was within twenty feet of the door. I never had seen any ghosts or spirits and I didn't believe in them. Yet, whenever I looked down, I could see the dead bandit from whom I had taken the hat. He was lying just as he was four hours before with his eyes glared wide open with his shaggy black blood-stained beard with flies swarming around his face. I could smell the fresh blood on the hat brim over my eyes. It made me feel a little strange.

"I was not anxious to meet any bandits away out there by myself, but I would have liked for a few to come that way so I could have fired on them and then get the best speed Old Ball had back to camp. They did not come and I had to stay my four hours—the longest four hours in my life. I wore the hat a long time, but I never did see the dead bandit again as I saw him that night.

"The next morning we started for Brownsville to attend the funeral of our dead Ranger. We got there early in the morning. A wagon had hauled in all the dead bandits, and they were unloaded in one pile on the public square. Here I saw the fat Mexican that I got the hat from, and also the one I got the sash from in the dagger thicket. I asked the Captain if I could wear the hat and sash to the funeral. He said for me to wear both as a warning to all bandits not to cross to the Texas side of the river after cattle.

"Berry Smith was taken to the cemetery in a black hearse with two fine black horses hitched to it. The Rangers marched on foot, along with two companies of U. S. soldiers. People gathered from far and near to see our sixteen-year-old Ranger boy laid to rest. The U. S. regulars fired a farewell shot over his grave where he sleeps on the Texas bank of the Rio Grande."

CHAPTER XI

THE FIGHT AT LAS CUEVAS

AFTER the battle at Palo Alto Prairie five months went by and it was November before the Rangers had another clash with Cortinas' men. This was the fight at Las Cuevas, a Mexican village or ranch deep in the brush three miles from the Rio Grande near Rio Grande City. The lord of Las Cuevas was Juan Flores, who served Cortinas as a cattle thief. This taking cattle from Texas McNelly was determined to stop.

On November 20, 1875, General William Steele opened a telegram McNelly sent from Las Cuevas in Mexico. In part it read:

> I CROSSED THE RIVER ON THE EIGHTEENTH. ON THE NINE-
> TEENTH I MARCHED ON FAST TO LAS CUEVAS. KILLED FOUR
> MEN BEFORE REACHING THE RANCH AND FIVE AFTERWARDS.
> ON MY ARRIVAL FOUND ABOUT THREE HUNDRED MEN. AFTER A
> FEW SHOTS I RETREATED TO THE RIVER. . . . THE MEXICANS
> FOLLOWED ME AND CHARGED ME. THEY WERE REPULSED. . . .
> THE MEXICANS MADE SEVERAL ATTEMPTS TO DISLODGE US BUT
> FAILED. . . . THE MEXICANS IN MY FRONT ARE ABOUT FOUR
> HUNDRED. WHAT SHALL I DO?
>
> L. H. MCNELLY
> CAPT RANGERS

An ordinary man in a foreign country with thirty men facing four hundred would have known that the sensible thing to do was to get out as fast as he could. But McNelly was not an ordinary man.

Here is how McNelly happened to be in Mexico. On November 16, some federal soldiers learned that the Mexicans were driving a herd of stolen cattle towards Las Cuevas crossing. The troops arrived at the crossing to find the cattle going out on the opposite bank. The troops

[55]

could not follow the cattle into Mexico, but while they were waiting on the bank Captain McNelly rode into their camp. He had dispatched a messenger to his men who made a ride of sixty miles in five hours, led by Old Casuse. The exciting events that followed are best told by Ranger Bill Callicott:

"Captain McNelly was already there. He came to me and said, 'Bill, you go to that near ranch and get two or three muttons for supper. You boys cook and eat all the mutton you want, and broil a chunk for dinner tomorrow. You won't need any breakfast—it would make us too late getting over. Have everything ready by twelve tonight; we will start crossing by one. A Mexican will take us in a dugout that will hold four men. We will swim our horses one at a time. Loosen your flank girths, as a horse can't swim well with a tight flank girth. Take your guns in your hands so that if the horse drowns you won't lose your guns. Do as I tell you and be ready to start by twelve.'

"Captain McNelly went to see the U. S. army officer, hoping he would let the soldiers go with us into Mexico. When he came back, he said the soldiers could not go.

"He told us to get ready, that we were going over if we never came back. When we were in ranks, the Captain stepped out in front of us and said:

" 'Boys, you have followed me as far as I can ask you to unless you are willing to go farther. Some of us may get back, or maybe all of us will get back, but if any of you do not want to go with me, step aside. I don't want you to go unless you are willing to volunteer. You understand there is to be no surrender—we ask no quarter nor give any. If you don't want to go, step aside.'

"We all said, 'Captain, we will go.'

" 'All right, that's the way to talk. . . . I will take Casuse, Tom Sullivan and myself first. We will take Casuse's horse. Then I want Lieutenant Robinson, John Armstrong, Sergeant Hall and Sergeant George Orell to bring their horses, and the rest of you come as fast as you can.'

"When these five horses were over, the Captain said not to take any more horses because they bogged down and had to be pulled out with ropes. So we went three at a time in the leaky Mexican boat. By four o'clock we were all together again in Mexico.

[56]

" 'Boys,' the Captain said, 'the pilot tells me that Las Cuevas Ranch is picketed in with high posts set in the ground with bars for a gate. We will march single file by a cowtrail. The mounted men will go first. When we get to the ranch, the bars will be let down. I want the five men on horses to dash through the ranch yelling and shouting. The rest of us will close in behind and do the best we can. Kill all you see, except old men, women and children. These are my orders and I want them obeyed.'

"The Captain and the guide led the way down the cowtrail through underbrush and trees so thick you could not see a rabbit ten feet away.

"We reached the ranch just at daylight. The Captain halted us just before we got to the bars, walked up and down the line of thirty of us three miles in Mexico afoot, and looked each man in the face.

" 'Boys, I like your looks. You are the palest set of men I ever looked at. That is a sign that you are going to do good fighting.'

"When the bars were let down, the Captain said:

" 'All you boys except Casuse stand aside. Casuse has not had a chance to breathe Mexican air or give a yell in Mexico for over twenty years. We'll let Casuse wake them up. Go through,' said the Captain.

"Casuse pushed his hat to the back of his head, drew his pistol, rammed both spurs to his old paint horse, gave a Comanche yell, and away the five went shooting and yelling. It was between daylight and sunup. The rest of us closed in behind them, and if the angels of heaven had come down on that ranch, the Mexicans would not have been more surprised.

"Many of the men were on their woodpiles cutting wood while their wives were cooking breakfast on little fires out of doors. We killed all we saw at the ranch.

"Then the pilot told the Captain we had hit the wrong ranch! Las Cuevas was a half mile up the trail.

" 'Well,' said the Captain, 'You all have given my surprise away. Take me to Las Cuevas as fast as you can.'

"We hurried on, and at Las Cuevas we saw 250 soldiers (McNelly said there were 300) dash into the ranch. We formed a line and opened fire at 150 yards. The Mexicans were shooting at us from behind houses, but their bullets went wild over our heads.

[57]

"Captain McNelly said it would be suicide for us to charge them—spell death to all of us and do no good. He told us to go back to the river.

"We hit the trail the way we came. As we passed Cachattus ranch there was nothing but the dead, and they lay where they fell, on the woodpiles and in the streets or roads. The women and children and old men were all gone.

"We went back to the river and put out pickets to await the coming of the Mexicans.

"Suddenly we heard yelling and shooting towards the pickets, and pretty soon Lieutenant Robinson jumped his horse off the bank almost on top of us. Lieutenant Armstrong and Sergeant George Orell lost their horses and came in on foot. We now had only three horses.

"We hid under the bank, and when the Mexicans could not see us they thought we were swimming the river. Here they came, twenty-five horsemen led by General Juan Flores, owner of Las Cuevas.

" 'Charge them, boys,' said the Captain.

"We ran up the cowtrail and formed a line.

" 'Open up on them as fast as you can!' said the Captain.

"We opened and they ran back to the thicket, but General Juan Flores fell dead from his horse with his pistol in his hand and two needle-gun bullets in his body.

"We formed a line four feet apart, marching and firing into the thicket until we came to where General Juan Flores lay. The Captain picked up the pistol. It was a Smith & Wesson, plated with gold and silver, the finest I ever saw. The Captain placed the pistol in his belt and we went back to the river."

We will interrupt Bill Callicott here to explain the situation that McNelly was in.

McNelly had thirty men hidden under the bank. During the day some soldiers joined them, but withdrew to Texas before night. The Mexicans sent a white flag and asked for a truce. McNelly agreed to cease fire for the night if the Mexicans would return the two horses with saddles and bridles that the pickets had lost, and he told them he could give them an hour's notice before he "commenced active operations." The horses were returned.

But let Bill Callicott tell the story of the last night in Mexico:

"The Captain brought us some bread stuff and told us to eat our mutton we had broiled.

" 'Boys, it's all off,' he said. 'The U. S. Captain won't let us have any of his men. But we will stay here a while. They can't cut us off from forage and water, and they can't cut us off from grub.'

"The Captain did not like the place where we were because the bank was too high. We moved to another place where the bank was about four feet with a slope to the water. He got two spades and stepped off a trench forty feet long fronting Mexico. He called three boys and said:

" 'I want this trench dug two feet deep and three feet wide; pile the dirt and pack it level. When the Mexicans charge, they will come in big numbers. We will fight them as they come from the thicket to the bank. If we can't stand them off at the bank, we will fall back to this trench and fight them to the death finish. . . . Now work. I will have three fresh men on every hour until it is finished.'

"If ever you saw boys scatter dirt we did, for well we knew if the Mexicans did charge over that bank that trench would be our death cell.

"When we finished, the Captain came and looked at our work and said the Confederates couldn't have done any better in the way of trench digging.

"After dark the Captain came to me and said:

" 'Bill, it is your time to go on guard. . . . I am going to put you in that bloodweed patch about one hundred yards from the Mexican line. When I get you to the place, I will press you on the shoulder and you sit down facing the Mexicans and keep a lookout. If one man comes towards the river halt him three times. If he does not stop, shoot him and come to me at the river. Be sure you let him get close enough so you won't miss him.'

"I still had on the hat I took off the dead bandit in the Palo Alto fight. I had been on guard about an hour; had seen nothing or heard nothing. Then I heard dry bloodweeds breaking towards the Mexican lines. The night was bright with starlight and finally I saw the object and took it for a man. It came closer, but I could not see it clearly for the bloodweeds. It was very near. I said 'Halt!' I said 'Halt' again, but it came on and I felt my Mexican hat begin to rise on my head as I sat there expecting a thousand Mexicans to charge me. Just then it turned to the left and I saw it was nothing but a cow. My Mexican hat settled down in place, but I could feel my heart thumping right under my collar. Soon the Captain came with the relief and I returned with him to the river."

Again we interrupt Bill Callicott to tell what happened the next day. Captain McNelly sent the telegram quoted at the first of the chapter. The Mexicans still did not know how many men McNelly had, and they were no doubt held back by the knowledge that if they attacked McNelly, the U. S. soldiers would fire on them from the Texas bank. At four o'clock in the afternoon, McNelly sent the Mexicans word that if they did not deliver the cattle, he would attack. This was a bluff, but it worked, and the Mexicans agreed to deliver the cattle the next day at Rio Grande City.

Now Bill Callicott continues his story:

"The next morning (November 21, 1875) the Captain took ten of us and went to Rio Grande City to get the cattle. They did not come till four o'clock. And when they did come, the Mexicans stopped on the Mexican side of the river. The Captain sent them word to bring them over. They sent word back that they couldn't cross the cattle until they were inspected. The Captain said, 'Well, boys, we are in it again.' There were twenty-five Mexicans with the cattle and ten of us. The Captain said, 'Well, boys, twenty-five to ten. That's near enough. We will go over again, if we never come back. What do you say?'

" 'We are with you, Captain,' we replied.

"A Mexican had a ferry. The Captain said, 'All Aboard!'

"The Mexicans had seventy-five head rounded up in a close herd. The twenty-five Mexicans were armed with Winchesters and pistols. They left the cattle and came over to us. They stopped in ten feet of us.

"The Captain told Tom Sullivan (interpreter) to tell them that the Presidente had promised to deliver the cattle to the Texas bank.

"The boss shook his head, and said not until they were inspected.

"The Captain told Tom to tell him they were stolen without being inspected and they could be driven back without it.

"The boss shook his head and said no.

"The Captain then told Tom to tell the boss that if they did not deliver the cattle in five minutes he would kill them all. He would have done it, too, for he had his red feather raised.

"If ever you saw cattle put across the river in a hurry, those Mexicans

[61]

did. They put across all but one, and she was so exhausted she could not take the water. We roped her and pulled her on the ferry and the Captain gave her to the Mexican boatmen for taking us over and bringing us back."

McNelly's work was about over. The exertions to which he drove himself were too much for his delicate frame. He died of tuberculosis at Burton September 4, 1877, a little less than two years after the Las Cuevas fight. He was then only thirty-three years of age. There has never been a greater Ranger or a more fearless man. His men worshipped him, as this final judgment by Bill Callicott will show:

"Captain McNelly was a man who seldom got mad and never did get excited. He always handled his men as a father would his children. I never heard him speak a cross word to one of them, but when he gave a command it had to be obeyed. Something came up the night after we got the cattle that showed how he felt toward us. After we penned the cattle, we went to the U. S. fort to get some forage for our horses. Captain McNelly and the U. S. Captain were sitting on a wagon tongue discussing the trip into Mexico. One of the Rangers went up and sat down by our Captain. The U. S. Captain jumped up and said:

" 'Captain McNelly, do you allow your privates to sit down by you?'

" 'Yes, sir,' said the Captain, 'I do at any time. I haven't a man in my company but what can lie down and sleep with me if he wants to do so.' "

CHAPTER XII

MAJOR JONES AND THE FRONTIER BATTALION

AJOR JOHN B. JONES was about five feet eight and weighed about 160 pounds. He was the sort of man you would look at twice, and had he not been weather-tanned, you would think he was a lawyer or businessman. He had regular features, a fine forehead, and piercing black eyes, with hair and mustache as dark as a raven's wing. He wore clothes of the best quality with white shirt and black string tie. The word dapper has been applied to him. He was born in South Carolina, December 22, 1834. His father had moved to Texas and was in the ranching business near Corsicana in Navarro County. Like Captain McNelly, Major Jones had seen service in the Civil War on the side of the Confederacy, and rose from private to captain.

He had a great love for horses, and engaged in raising them—the finest that could be obtained. "As a horseman, I have never seen his equal," wrote his niece. "His steed and himself seemed to be one—in perfect rhythm and harmony in every movement. He was simply irresistible on horseback, and such lovely and high-spirited horses as he always rode, usually a deep bay or shining mahogany. . . . How well I remember those magnificent stallions. I always remember them with gold rosettes and fluttering ribbons at their ears—Gold Eye, Dellenger, Lion, and the equally splendid brood mares."

It was May 2, 1874, that the oversized governor of Texas, Richard Coke, handed to the undersized, dashing ex-Confederate a commission making him Major of the Frontier Battalion. Within thirty days Major Jones had five companies organized and in the field, strung out along the western frontier from Red River almost to the Rio Grande. He had the right to hire and fire the men, and he would put up with no foolishness from the adventure-loving and often irresponsible youths who thought they would like to go a-rangering. He was firm without being harsh, and, as soon as the men knew he meant business, they came to respect him as their leader. He did not command from an office but from the field. He usually travelled with an escort consisting of an ambulance and a small squad of horsemen. He patrolled "down the line" and up again, visiting all five companies, tightening the discipline, and directing the activities. Each man had his horse and blanket, and even when in camp, which might boast a few tents, the men usually slept on the ground. Each Ranger had the tools of his trade—a rifle and a Colt revolver. Each furnished his own horse, but if a horse was lost in the service the state would pay for it. The Rangers have never worn uniforms, and there was none in the Frontier Battalion. The garb of the Ranger was good boots on his feet, a good hat on his head, and whatever he chose to wear in between. Around his waist he wore a belt from which hung his holster and in which he carried a supply of cartridges.

A company would set up headquarters in charge of a captain, and there would be one corporal and one sergeant. The men prepared their own food over a campfire, and by our standards it would leave something to be desired. Men who exercise and live in the open, such as cowboys and Texas Rangers, crave no great variety of food. They want plenty of meat, which the Rangers could get from wild game or a fat yearling belonging to some ranchman, and next to this they want plenty of bread and coffee—especially coffee. Sourdough biscuits were cooked in Dutch ovens, meat over an open fire or in another oven, and there was sure to be a black iron pot full of beans seasoned with red pepper, molasses, and side bacon. Men who ate such fare and rode horses all day were thin of flank, strong, wiry, and of wonderful endurance.

Major Jones commanded the Frontier Battalion from 1874 until 1879. He was forty years old when he organized this remarkable corps of Rangers, and he was only forty-six when he died. When we remember that Captain McNelly died at the age of thirty-three, we may suspect that these men really gave their lives so that Texas might have peace.

It was under Major Jones and Captain McNelly that the Ranger force reached the peak of its performance. Never before or since have the men had so much to do or done it better. It seemed that the enemy was at every gate. The bandits and cow thieves were wrecking the Rio Grande valley, the Indians were ravaging the western border, and white outlaws were depredating on the people within the settlements. Therefore it is no exaggeration to say that those Rangers—McNelly's and Jones'—were fighting on three fronts. We have already told of what McNelly did. Now here is what was the work of the Frontier Battalion commanded by the little major.

On July 12, 1874 Lieutenant Wilson rode in to the Salt Creek camp from a scout to report that he had found a fresh Indian trail. Twenty-four men and three officers, including Major Jones, set off on the trail which they followed easily. The Indians led the way toward the mountains and entered Lost Valley, where their number was increased by fifty warriors, bringing their number to a hundred men. It must be re-

membered that these Rangers had just been called out, were inexperienced, and allowed themselves to be drawn into a trap. The Indians scattered through the mountains and took concealed positions, where they could look down on the Rangers as they rode into the narrow valley, which offered little cover. By this date the Indians had guns as well as bows and arrows, and were able to hold the white men at bay. All day long the Rangers were surrounded. Two men, D. W. H. Bailey and W. A. Glass, went for water, were cut off by Indians, and killed. Two others, Lee Corn and George Moore, were wounded. The mountains were so steep and the valley so narrow that the Indians rolled rocks from the hills down on the white men.

Half of the Rangers' horses had been killed, and that meant that the whole party could not escape even if the way had been open. The Rangers decided to stand their ground through the night and send a rider to Jacksboro where some soldiers were stationed. The man who ordinarily would have undertaken this ride was Lee Corn, who lived in Jacksboro and knew the way there. But Lee Corn had been wounded and could not ride. Lee had a tough range horse who knew the country

and would find his way home to Jacksboro even though his rider did not know the country. Everything depended on the horse.

When a Ranger—and unfortunately we do not know his name—volunteered to make the ride on Lee Corn's horse, Lee told him to point the horse's nose towards Jacksboro and let the horse find the way. The messenger got through and a United States army captain arrived at Lost Valley with a squad of Negro troops before daylight.

Indians avoid night fighting. They knew that help might come to the Rangers with daylight, and so they stole away in the darkness. The soldiers and Rangers went out to hunt for them the next morning, but they had scattered, leaving no trail. The Rangers captured one horse, a quantity of bows and arrows, and moccasins. Major Jones said the warriors had breech-loading guns, which were still not too common, and it was with these that they had killed a dozen Ranger horses. The two dead men were rolled in blankets and carried to Jacksboro for burial; the two wounded men were left at Jacksboro for medical care.

The fight at Lost Valley was a bad start for the Frontier Battalion.

More men were killed and wounded and more horses lost here than in any Indian fight after that time. It is probable that the Rangers learned a good lesson and became more wary after Lost Valley.

By the end of July Major Jones had patrolled the whole line from south to north and was ready for the return trip. By October he had visited each company three times. He had improved discipline, let the captains know that they were to stay in the field and not in the towns, and that furloughs should not be requested without good reason. He set up a courier system with messengers riding the line from one camp to another to carry news and to watch for trails made by raiding parties that might come into the settlements.

At the end of six months, Major Jones reported that the Rangers had had fifteen fights with Indians, killed fifteen, wounded ten, captured one, followed twenty-eight trails, and recovered two hundred head of cattle and seventy-five head of horses. In the second six months, twenty raiding parties came, there were five fights, five Indians were killed and one wounded. In the third six-months period only six bands of Indians came, and there was one fight. In the next six months the border was free of raids. So, within two years of the time Major Jones had formed his Frontier Battalion, the border had been cleared. Rangers had gone to the fartherest boundaries of Texas and beyond to end the threat of the red men. Thus ends the saga of the red man in Texas.

CHAPTER XIII

GEORGE W. ARRINGTON AND THE BLIZZARD RIDE

O N Christmas day, 1878, George W. Arrington became captain of Company C. He had been three years in the service, had made the rank of sergeant, and had gained the respect and confidence of Major Jones. "I have," wrote Major Jones to General Steele, "tested him thoroughly in the management of men, in command-ing detachments, and in his capacity for business, and think him well qualified for this business." He was thirty-four years old when he got his commission.

George Arrington was born in Alabama, entered the Confederate army at the age of sixteen, and became a member of Mosby's guerrillas. He had some trouble with the carpetbaggers in Alabama after the war, and he left for Mexico to join the army of the Mexican emperor, Maxi-milian. After Maximilian's execution, Arrington went to Central Amer-ica, but later turned up in Texas. He seems to have had a good reason for leaving Alabama, and for not going back. At any rate, he never let his people there know where he was until he had become a Ranger captain and one of the most respected citizens of Texas.

Captain Arrington was hot-headed. His training in the Civil War, where he fought most of the time inside the enemy lines, had made him stern and unyielding in discipline. Major Jones recognized this, and warned him not to be too strict with his men until they had learned to obey him.

His first duty as a Ranger captain was along the line of stations Major Jones had set up, but here instead of hunting Indians he spent most of his time hunting white outlaws and murderers. In May he went to San Saba to protect an attorney who had killed a saloon-keeper over an election dispute. "I found the entire community in a great state of excitement," he wrote, "and a mob nearly ready to do its dirty work. . . . I am camped in the Courthouse and have no fears of being attacked." In July he was at Fort Griffin where a band of gunmen under the leadership of John Larn and John Sellman were terrorizing the community by night riding and firing their guns at the doors of the settlers. A citizen mob gathered and hanged John Larn, and it would have hanged Sellman had he not been warned by a woman named Hurricane Minnie.

As winter came on, Indians were reported in the Panhandle, which lay far west of the line of settlement. On New Year's Day, 1879, Captain Arrington started a scout in the Pease River country. The Rangers were snowed in for several days on the O'Brien ranch, but on January 15 they attacked a small party of Indians, killing one. They then struck a camp of fourteen lodges and 150 ponies. Just as the Rangers were about to separate the Indians from their horses, a party of nine soldiers from the Tenth Cavalry interfered, saying that the Indians were under their protection. This action infuriated Captain Arrington, who did not believe that any Indians should be allowed in Texas.

The next spring Captain Arrington went to Wheeler County, where friction had developed between the soldiers at Fort Elliott and the citizens.

Soon after Arrington arrived at Fort Elliott he had a clash with Colonel J. W. Davidson.

Davidson wanted to know what Arrington's orders were in regard to Indians. Would he attack them? Would he kill them if he found any?

"I replied that I most assuredly would if they were armed."

Later Arrington was told that Colonel Davidson had said that if the Rangers killed or molested the Indians, he would order the U. S. soldiers to fire on the Texas Rangers. Arrington refused to be bluffed. He wrote Colonel Davidson on June 18 demanding to know if the army officer had made any such threat. Davidson did not answer the letter, but let the matter drop.

Arrington moved farther west and visited Colonel Charles Goodnight who had set up the first ranch in the Panhandle.

The Rangers were now on the very edge of an unknown country extending through the Panhandle and into the deserts of New Mexico. They spent several months scouting, learning the location of scattered water holes and other landmarks. They found shallow lakes, bearing such names as Double Lakes, Cedar Lake, Rich Lake, and Silver Lake. These lakes were little more than buffalo wallows.

Arrington knew that the Indians came from the west across the unknown country, onto the High Plains where a few settlers had now ventured. Arrington said to himself that there must be water out there, for even an Indian cannot cross that great waste without water for himself and his horse. This mythical water that he hoped to find, he called the Lost Lake.

Arrington decided to go in search of the Lost Lakes. He went in the dead of winter. No mariner ever set out to sea with more careful preparations than the Rangers made for this journey. Arrington ordered his wagons to Double Lakes and set up a temporary camp in the Yellow House caves. He secured two buffalo hides fashioned like saddlebags. Into these he placed four ten-gallon water kegs to be carried by two pack-mules. The party set out on January 12, 1880, and camped the first night at Silver Lake.

"My plan," Arrington said, "was to make a two days' march from Silver Lake in a due southwest course into the desert, hoping . . . to intersect the Indian trail we had left at Double Lakes and possibly to find the Lost Lakes, which tradition said were somewhere out there in the desert. I believed that by steady marching for twelve hours a day I could within two days make from 80 to 100 miles, and if I failed to find water within that time, I intended to fill all canteens from the four kegs of water we had with us, and give the remainder to the horses and re-trace my steps.

"At sunrise (January 13, 1880) we fell in line and taking our course by a small compass we started at a brisk walk into the unknown region. . . . At the end of about thirty miles march, we came suddenly in sight of the real desert. This consisted of low sandhills, extending north, south and west as far as the eye, aided by powerful field glasses, could discern, absolutely barren of vegetation, almost white as snow; certainly by far the most desolate and uninviting region I ever beheld.

"We knew the reputation of this desolate region for bewildering the brain, choking the throat, parching the lips, and swelling the tongue of man and beast, . . . but we did not swerve from our course. We approached it, plunged into it, and traveled on and on.

"Night came on, with not the slightest change in the face of the surrounding country, and we camped in one of the wildest and most desolate spots imaginable. . . . On the following morning, as soon as it was light enough to see the needle on the face of the compass, we were again on the march. The sun came up and as it climbed higher and higher and cast its glistening rays down upon the white sands, we were entertained continually with nature's most wonderful picture show, the Desert Mirage.

"Miles away appeared a lake of water, on whose margin stood beautiful groves of trees, so natural that one could scarcely believe they were not real; but the picture would only last for a moment, when the scene would shift, change, and finally disappear. . . .

"All the day long we held our steady course, never varying, with only the billowy white sand extending in every direction, the whole pervaded by an awful silence—a silence that you could almost hear. The stillness seemed to affect the men and not a dozen words were exchanged among them during the day."

[74]

THE DRY SALT LAKE

About sunset of the second day the Rangers approached a hill and noted that their tired horses were on firmer ground. At the top of the hill they saw beyond and below a dry salt lake. Captain Arrington had learned that all springs in that country issue from the west, and so he and his men rode around the lake looking anxiously for water. What they found was brackish, but it was water, good for the tired and thirsty horses. There were many signs of Indians, for this was the water supply for the Indians traveling from New Mexico into Texas. There were ashes of many campfires, and skeletons of horses that had been killed for food.

What interested the Rangers most was an Indian sign board. This was the broad fan-shaped shoulder bone of a giant buffalo, bleached white, standing upright from the ground. On it the Indians had "written" their messages in green, yellow and red. On the left edge of this bleached bone were some Indian tepees, trees, and an Indian standing over a campfire. Another Indian was approaching this camp, leading a pony with a travois loaded with baggage. (The travois was made by lashing the ends of two poles to a horse and letting the other ends drag on the ground to form a platform for a rawhide net on which Indian baggage could be carried from place to place.) Behind the Indian and the pony, at the extreme right, were horse tracks, and the significant feature here was that the *horses wore shoes*. The Rangers took this sign board to mean that the Indians had gone to a place where there were trees, and that they had left because men on shod horses, meaning white men, were coming after them.

The Rangers spent the night here, and gave the scant water they found the name of Ranger Lake. On the next day, which was January 16, they moved farther west where they found four more lakes, a real camping place where the Indians had killed many cattle. The bones were everywhere, and each skull had a round hole in it from which the Indians had removed the brains to use in tanning hides or to eat.

Returning to Ranger Lake, Captain Arrington secreted his men in the hills to await the Indians. The Rangers lay in the hills for fifteen days. Their food ran low and they went on half-rations of bacon, flour and coffee without sugar. Then the bacon gave out, and they had to kill antelope for meat. The Indians did not put in their appearance, probably because their scouts observed the actions of the white men.

On the last day of January, the Rangers broke camp and started their return march. The day was fair and sunny, but about five o'clock on the morning of February 1, a blizzard struck, and by the time the men took to their saddles, the ground was covered with snow. Could men practically without food, and on worn-out horses, make their way over a sandy desert from which snow had erased all landmarks? Could they hope to reach the shelter of the Yellow Houses? Those questions had to be answered.

"It would," wrote Captain Arrington, "be hard to imagine a more forlorn aspect than the little squad of men and horses presented that morning as they fell in line and took up march facing that terrible blizzard, already half-famished with not a morsel of food. The horses, almost exhausted, reeled as they walked. The men gaunt and haggard from starvation, their faces drawn and pinched until their most intimate friends would not have recognized them.

"I knew that 50 or 60 miles northeast was the Yellow Houses and Causey Brothers Buffalo Camp and that there was relief if we could reach these points. But I also knew that if we should miss these points, there was little chance for us in this terrible storm. I got my course as best I could and struck out facing the storm with the men and pack-mules following. Those who know anything about a blizzard on the north plains of Texas may have some idea of my situation. The snow by this time was twelve or fifteen inches deep."

The February days are short, and night came with the men far from their goal. During the night one of the Rangers' horses gave out. There was no horse in the party strong enough to carry two men, but fortunately Captain Arrington had picked up an Indian pony that could

be used. But the Ranger was so exhausted that he collapsed and could not mount the horse. The other men tied him on the pony, and the procession moved on through the stormy night.

Finally, the clouds broke and a single star appeared in the cold sky, right in front of the half-frozen men. Shortly the clouds dissolved and the sky was filled with the cold bright points of thousands of heavenly bodies, but the first star was the most important. Arrington took it as a guide, followed it, and finally came to the sheltering breaks of a canyon. The half-frozen men and horses dropped off the plain into the precious shelter, and found that they *had hit the Yellow Houses, near where they had left their wagon.* In one of the caves of the canyon they started a fire, cutting up a packsaddle to use as kindling. The next morning, February 3, men were sent with pack-mules to bring food from Causey Brothers' Buffalo Camp, but the men were so hungry and weak that they were allowed to eat only a little at a time. The next day the Rangers moved on to Camp Roberts, where they arrived February 6. They had been gone twenty-five days and had marched over eight hundred miles.

The story of this expedition holds within it a clue to the importance of the Ranger captain. A man less resolute than Arrington would not have made the trip in the dead of winter, and under a man less able the expedition would have ended in stark disaster. It was Arrington who provided for the water and determined the line of march and the direction. It was such men as Arrington, who might have been called, in a more romantic era, the Iron-Handed, who built the tradition of the force. Major Jones was proud of him and considered him one of his best captains.

CHAPTER XIV

END OF THE INDIAN TRAIL

T WAS on August 2, 1879, that Lieutenant George W. Baylor left San Antonio for El Paso, nearly six hundred miles away. Baylor's party consisted of two heavy wagons, a mule-drawn ambulance, and a mounted guard of six Rangers. One wagon carried household goods, including a square piano, a game rooster, and four hens. In the ambulance was Mrs. Baylor, her sister, and her two daughters, age eight and fourteen. In the escort was young J. B. Gillett, who would later marry one of these daughters. Thus did civilization and law go west. The party was forty-two days on the road, arriving at Ysleta near El Paso in September.

Baylor was forty-seven years old, six feet two in height, and had a fair education. He had taken the place of Lieutenant Tays, whom we shall meet in the Salt War. Baylor was a courageous and fearless fighter, but as a Ranger officer he would not rank with either McNelly or Arrington.

Baylor had been in El Paso less than a month when an Indian raid was reported.

The last Apache raids into Texas were led by Chief Victorio, who quit the reservation in New Mexico in the fall of 1879, with 125 warriors and 100 women and children. Victorio's scouts knew the rugged country on both sides of the Rio Grande, knew where the water holes were, and where to find grass for the horses and wood for the camp fires. From the candle-like peaks known as the Candelarias, he sent raiding parties into two nations.

Six or seven of his horse thieves stole a herd of ponies from the

Mexican village of San Jose. Fifteen Mexicans followed the trail, only to be ambushed by Victorio as they entered the mountains, where all were killed. Thirty-five more Mexicans went to see what had happened —all the men in the village of Carrajal—and all of them were killed in the same manner.

Panic ran wild down the border, and the Mexicans sent for the Texas Rangers to join in an all-out effort to drive Victorio and his Apaches away. A mixed army of border fighters took the trail and came to the pass where the Apaches had ambushed and slaughtered the Mexicans. Baylor described the scene in this letter to Major Jones:

"The scene of the conflict was perfectly horrible. I saw in one little narrow parapet which the . . . Mexicans had hastily thrown up seven men piled in a space 6 x 7 feet. The Indians had shown great cunning,

as they have through all this campaign. The trail passed between, and [was] commanded by, three rocky peaks. The Mexicans were fired on from one side just as they reached the crest of the mountains. They had evidently dismounted and ran into the rocks on the opposite side when the Indians began killing the horses. . . . They were all killed. A letter written by them asking for help was found outside their breastwork near the body [bodies] of two men who had evidently attempted to escape but were riddled with balls." Twenty-six bodies were buried at this place. Victorio and his Apaches had disappeared in the Mexican mountains, and pursuit was without result.

Victorio's raids continued until October 14, 1880, when General Terrasas attacked Victorio in Chihuahua, killed the chief, sixty warriors, and eighteen women, and took sixty-eight prisoners. Three months later,

the last fight between the Texas Rangers and the Indians brought the curtain down and closed forever the long and bloody chapter of Indian wars.

After Victorio's death, what remained of his band scattered, and at times some of them were reported in Texas. Early in January of 1881 they attacked the stage in Quitman Canyon, killed the driver and a gambler who was a passenger. Major Jones wired Baylor to investigate and on January 16 Baylor set out on the last Indian campaign. From Quitman Canyon the Indians fled south into the Big Bend and crossed

into Mexico at the Hot Springs. On the trail the Rangers found the gambler's kid glove, the stage driver's boot top, a pair of moccasins, blankets, saddles, baskets, two dead horses, and a dead mule. The Indians had killed these animals for food, had drawn the blood in vessels, and left a mule tongue stewing when they fled. They left a five gallon can of mescal, an alcoholic drink made from native plants, and fifteen gallons more in a horsehide sunk in the ground. The Rangers followed the trail towards Eagle Mountains, found it, lost it, found it leading on to Chili Peak, Rattlesnake Springs, to the edge of the Sierra Diabolos, or Devil's Mountains.

Flying doves told them water was near, and they knew the Indians could not pass water in such a dry country. The Rangers made a dry camp, without water, fire, or food. Before daylight January 29, 1881, the Rangers set out on the trail, which led north over a rocky crest from which the Indian campfires could be seen below.

The Rangers came within gunshot without being discovered. The Indians were just getting out of bed, and the sun was just beginning to show over the distant mountains. They knelt in hiding and took dead aim to send the leaden bullets among the Apaches. The Indians made no resistance, but ran each for himself. As the warriors went first, the women and children suffered most. A squaw and two children were captured. The woman and the smallest child, a mere baby, were wounded. Nevill reported that everytime the baby heard a gunshot it would scream. Why not? Since men and women all wore blankets, it was impossible to tell one from the other. Baylor said that under the law governing the Frontier Battalion it was not necessary to make any distinction. The Rangers killed four warriors, two women, and two children, and wounded many more. They captured seven mules, nine horses, two Winchesters, one Remington carbine, a U. S. cavalry pistol, six cavalry saddles, an American saddle, a Mexican saddle, and 150 yards of calico. The Rangers piled such Indian plunder as they did not want to keep, including pack-saddles, and built a bonfire on Diabolo Mountain to celebrate their victory and the end of an era.

Here also the Rangers put new fuel on the Indian campfire and made breakfast. That meal was described thus by Captain Baylor: "We took breakfast on the ground occupied by the Indians, which all enjoyed as we had eaten nothing since dinner the day before. Some of the men found horsemeat pretty good, while others found venison and mescal good enough. We had almost a boundless view from our breakfast table: toward the north the grand old Cathedral Peak of the Guadalupe Mountains; further west the San Antonio Mountains, the Cornudas,

Las Almas, Sierra Alta; at the Hueco Tanks, only twenty-four miles from our headquarters, the Eagle Mountains. The beauty of the scenery (was) only marred by man's inhumanity to man, the ghostly forms of the Indians lying around."

This celebration on the lofty mountain overlooking the mysterious desert could be packed with symbolism. The place was the Devil Mountain, a place where an era ended, centuries of war between the white man and the red. The coffee the Rangers drank that morning might have gagged less hardy men, for in it was mixed the blood of the last Texas-slain Indians. The camp was by two little water holes, and the killed and the wounded Indians had left their blood in the water. As is often the case in war, the toast to victory is nearly always laced with blood. But the Indian wars were over.

RANGERS IN QUEST OF A DOG

Shortly after Baylor's Rangers returned from the expedition into Mexico after Victorio, some of the men were camped about one hundred miles east of El Paso. One day two mining engineers, J. P. Andrews and W. P. Wiseall, drove into the camp. They were on the road from Colorado to San Antonio, and made inquiry of the Rangers as to the best route they should take to the next settlements which were on the Pecos seventy-five miles to the east. The engineers had a new ambulance, drawn by good horses, a fine saddle horse, and the best firearms. What interested the Rangers most, however, was a beautiful shepherd dog, well-trained to obey his master.

Against the advice of the Rangers, the engineers followed the old Butterfield stage route which led by Heuco Tanks, Alamo Springs, the Coronudas, and Crow Flats. Along this trail fragments of Victorio's Apaches were lurking, lying in wait for just such travelers.

The engineers made it to Crow Flats and were camped in an abandoned stage station, where the Apaches found them and drove off their horses. They were afoot seventy-five miles from the Pecos settlements, one hundred miles west to the Rangers at Ysleta.

They tried for the Pecos. To deceive the Indians, they rigged up two dummies and left them "on guard," and to give the place the appearance of being inhabited, they left the dog, knowing that he would sound the alarm when anyone approached the camp. Providing the dog with water, side bacon, and a sack of corn, they ordered him to stand guard, and set off early in the night. Daylight found them twenty-five miles away in the Guadalupe Mountains. Here they were attacked by the Apaches. By taking refuge in the peaks of the mountains, the engineers stood off the Indians all day, but as night approached, they knew they could not last much longer.

They escaped by one of those strange incidents that occur when men are ready to act quickly when an advantage appears. One Indian had approached very near and concealed himself behind a boulder. It was about dark when the watchers saw a thick mop of hair appear over the boulder. When the rifles cracked, the Indian went down, the boulder was dislodged, and started rolling down the mountain, thundering against other boulders, crashing through cedar, opening an unexpected way of escape. The engineers ran after the boulder, by the trail it had left, by the kicking warrior, and into the night. When daylight came, they were back at the stage station where they found the dog still on guard.

The fifty-mile walk had worn out their shoes and left the men exhausted. They rested, ate, and discussed what they would use for shoes on the hundred-mile walk to El Paso. The only thing available was some gunny sacks. They wrapped their feet in these, tied them with thongs, took along some spares, put out more feed for the dog, and set off for a hundred-mile walk over a mountainous desert.

On January 18, 1880, Andrews and Wiseall walked into the Ysleta Ranger camp more dead than alive, minus all equipment save their guns, clothes in shreds, their feet torn and bleeding.

Their first thought was about their dog. Would the Rangers go get this faithful animal? There doubtless was a good deal of discussion. Rangers were sent to this wild country to protect people, not dogs.

The result of the discussion was that early one morning eight men under command of Sergeant J. B. Gillett saddled their horses, tied their food to the saddles, and set out on a hundred-mile ride through a dangerous country to rescue a dog.

The nine Rangers were gone a week. They found the dog still on guard. He did not know that these strange men coming on horseback were his friends. He set up a great commotion. He had been told to keep off all comers and now he faced the Rangers from the top of the wall, hackles up, teeth bared. For fifteen days he had been alone. Finally, the Rangers persuaded him that they were his friends, and then he was as joyous as he had been vicious. He wagged his tail, he whined, he cavorted, he showed his fine teeth in that happy grin that often is seen on the face of a happy dog. He had not had an easy time. He had fought off the coyotes and other varmints, eaten all the bacon, and most of the corn. He had stood the siege of the desert.

[86]

CHAPTER XV

THE BOOK OF WANTED MEN

IN CHASING the red men beyond the border, the Rangers had left the white settlements behind. The western half of Texas was unoccupied, save for an occasional ranch.

This vast vacant country, freed from Indians but not settled by white people, was a safe hiding place for fugitives. There was no law in all that country. Along the border of settlement, which ran north and south through the center of the state, the outlaws congregated. They robbed travelers, held up stages, stole horses and cattle, formed gangs to intimidate whole communities, and occasionally fell out and fought among themselves. Once the Rangers had finished with the Indians, they turned their attention to the wild gentry of this region.

In reporting the work of the Rangers for the first six months, Major Jones said: "Besides scouting for Indians, the Battalion has rendered much service to the people by breaking up bands of desperadoes who had established themselves in these thirty (border) counties." In August of 1876, a little more than two years after the Frontier Battalion took the field, General William Steele wrote Major Jones that lawlessness by white people was becoming more important than Indian raids. There were so many outlaws loose in the country that General Steele was preparing a directory of wanted men. He had 3000 names, and more were coming in every mail. This directory of criminals—thieves, murderers, and highwaymen—was published in book form and a copy sent to each Ranger captain.

In March of 1877 Major Jones sent the following orders to his men: "The operations of the companies will be directed, more than hitherto has been the case, to the suppression of lawlessness and crime, will be confined mostly to the sparsely settled frontier counties and to the particular localities through which cattle will be driven during the spring and summer."

Up to this time the Rangers had fought with their backs to the settlements; they had faced outward to fight invaders. Now they turned their horses' heads and their gun muzzles inward, to meet men of their own breed, nearly as intelligent and as well armed as they. The old

enemy from beyond the border had no friends within it, but the new foes had friends everywhere. While it was easy to recognize a Mexican or a Comanche or an Apache, it was hard to tell a white outlaw from a good citizen. The outlaw wore the same clothes, spoke the same language, carried the same arms, and enjoyed the same legal rights as the best citizen. In hunting criminals the Rangers became a little less the soldier and a little more the detective and police officer.

MAJOR JONES ON THE BORDER

There is no better way to get an idea of the new problem than to ride in our imagination with Major Jones as he made a tour among the lawless characters of the Texas border.

From Kerr County, July 1, 1875, Major Jones talking: "I am satisfied there is an extensive organization of thieves on this part of the frontier. . . . All the stolen stock has been taken out this way. The Leon Springs robbers were going in the direction of the head of the Llano. The white man who was wounded in the fight died near here. He confessed to being a member of an organized band of horse thieves and robbers. . . . Their camp is supposed to be in the vicinity of old Fort Terrett. I shall start tomorrow on a scout for them. . . . Will make a thorough search . . . and will break them up if they are there."

In September he was in Mason County, where a feud had broken out between the German settlers and the Americans. The Americans were threatening to "burn out the Dutch" because the Germans had taken the side of the North in the late Civil War. From Cold Springs Major Jones wrote: "I turned back down the road and remained at this place at sundown. I find the houses closed, a death-like stillness in the place and an evident suspense if not dread in the minds of the inhabitants. Every man is armed."

A German named Don Hoester had just been killed. A week earlier two men from the American faction had killed a man named Cheyney while he was preparing their breakfast and in the presence of his wife. Each side accused the other of causing trouble, and the Americans said they were coming to Mason to kill all the Dutch. Major Jones's answer was: "I immediately went down there with a detachment of men, succeeded in quieting their fears, prevailed on several who had run away to come back and stay home, and have kept a force there ever since until the last few days."

Letters were sent to the Governor in Austin accusing the Major. He never did learn which faction made the charge of taking sides. Jones replied that he had come in the interest of law and order, and that he had succeeded, because there had been peace and quiet since his arrival. He had acted in the best interest of all, and now it was time for him to move on, leaving a Ranger lieutenant in control of the situation.

Major Jones next struck at a band of Kimble County outlaws in their headquarters at Junction. He sent five detachments of Rangers to converge on the place suddenly. They made forty-two arrests for murder, theft, forgery, assault, escaped convicts, and suspicion. The grand jury returned twenty-five indictments, several against the sheriff and county judge. Both resigned. The trials were postponed because the commissioners could not find enough honest men to form a jury.

Major Jones said this working after outlaws was hard work, quite different from chasing Indians. The Rangers had to "shell the woods," take the outlaws, surround the houses at night and close in at dawn. The Rangers had to be more careful about killing outlaws than Indians because outlaws had "rights" and lawyers. Often the Rangers came in contact with the women-folk who gave them some terrible tongue-lashings. Finally, Major Jones said, he would have to go on up the line, but would leave a small detachment to keep the Kimble rascals from reorganizing and to run out any strays that had been missed.

One of the worst feuds on the frontier was raging around the town of Lampasas between the Horrell family on one side and the Mitchell

and Higgins families on the other. In the Horrell-Higgins feud, Thomas L. Horrell led one faction and J. P. (Pink) Higgins the other.

It is not clear just why the Horrells and Higgins decided to kill each other off to the last man. Apparently the trouble began in 1873 when some Negro police were sent to Lampasas. In a gunfight in a saloon the state police attempted to arrest a man named Bill Bowen. In the shooting scrape that followed, the captain of the troopers and two of his men lay dead, and Thomas and Martin Horrell were wounded.

On March 26, 1877, one of the Horrell boys rode into Lampasas to report that he and his brother had been ambushed and both wounded while coming in to court. For this they blamed the Higgins faction. In July a second outbreak occurred, and two men were killed and two wounded. On July 25 a man named Graham, who was supposed to belong to the Higgins factions, was shot and killed from ambush, and the Horrells were charged with the crime. Major Jones hurried to the scene of trouble with seven men—all he had.

Three days later, July 28, he struck at sunrise, and arrested fourteen members of the Horrell party at the home of Mart Horrell, ten miles from Lampasas. He released all but Tom, Mart, and Sam Horrell. There was great excitement, and many feared the Horrells would be released

by their friends or slain by their enemies. Three days later Major Jones had taken the three leaders of the Higgins faction, Pink Higgins, R. A. Mitchell, and W. R. Wren.

Major Jones now revealed his true genius as a law enforcement officer. This was his ability as a peace-maker, his skill in getting desperate men who were ready to kill each other to lay down their arms and talk sense. On August 2, 1877, Major Jones brought the two factions together, and on July 30, the three Horrells, who were prisoners, addressed a letter to the Higgins faction proposing peace. In part the letter read:

> From this standpoint, looking back over the past with its terrible experiences both to ourselves and to you; . . . we have determined to take the initiatory in a move for reconciliation. Therefore we present this paper in which we hold ourselves in honor bound to lay down our arms and to end the strife in which we have been engaged . . .
>
> PROVIDED:
> That you shall on your part take upon yourselves a similar obligation as respects our friends and us, and shall address a paper to us with your signatures thereon . . . Hoping that this may bring about the happy results which it aims at we remain.

The letter, written in Major Jones' hand, and witnessed by him, was signed by Thomas L., S. W., and C. O. M. Horrell—Tom, Sam, and Mart.

Three days later, August 2, Major Jones returned to the Horrells with the Higgins reply. This letter, written by Major Jones, and witnessed by him, read in part:

> Your favor . . . was handed to us by Major Jones. We have carefully noted its contents and approve most sincerely the spirit of communication. It would be difficult for us to express in words the mental disturbance to ourselves which the sad quarrel with its fatal consequences . . . occasioned. And now with passions cooled we look back with you sorrowfully to the past, and promise with you to commence at once . . . the task of repairing the injuries . . . as far as our power extends to do. . . . On our part we lay down our weapons with the honest purpose to regard the feud which has existed between us as a by gone thing . . . Furthermore . . . we will abstain from offering insult or injury to you or yours.

This letter was signed by J. P. Higgins, R. A. Mitchell, and W. R. Wren.

It took a man of rare gift to go into a feud such as this and persuade the men to agree to a truce. It is doubtful if the men on either side fully forgave their enemies, and it is certain that they continued to carry their weapons, because at that time and in that place nearly all men went armed. But the wise action of the little major brought temporary peace and freed the Rangers to turn their attention elsewhere.

SGT. ARMSTRONG'S EXPLOITS

In the process of thinning out the white criminals, we cannot overlook John B. Armstrong, one of McNelly's men. Even a brief recital of his acts will show that he was trained in the McNelly school, a man after McNelly's own heart. His field of operation lay south of Major Jones' line, near the Mexican border. One of the most famous outlaws in that region was King Fisher. In addition to terrorizing the country, he dealt in cattle and horses, many of which were stolen. Sergeant John B. Armstrong was sent into King Fisher's realm, and from Carrizo Springs made the following report to Captain McNelly on October 1, 1876.

"I was unable to reach Carrizo until last night. On my arrival I learned that a party of desperadoes were camped on the Espinoza Lake ten miles northeast of this place and that another party would pass the night at the Pendencia. I sent Corporal Williams with ten men and a number of citizens to the latter place. I started with the balance of the detachment for the camp of the Espinoza."

The Rangers reached the Espinoza about midnight. They left two men to guard the horses and a prisoner, and approached the camp but were discovered. Armstrong reported that "a lively little fight ensued, resulting in the death of three of them and the wounding of another in five places." While this fight was going on, the horses left with the two guards became excited, and the prisoner attempted to escape and was killed. A squad of three men was sent to arrest a "bad" Mexican at Whaley's camp, and reported that they had to kill him in self-defense. Like McNelly, Armstrong managed to take no prisoners that night. The parties killed at Espinoza had fifty head of stolen stock. King Fisher had been gone a week, with a large drove of cattle. Armstrong said, "You could not persuade a man in this whole country to testify against King Fisher or any of his clan."

Armstrong did take one prisoner, a very famous one. John Wesley Hardin was probably the champion murderer of Texas. He is said to have killed twenty-five or thirty men. On May 26, 1874, he killed Deputy Sheriff Charles Webb in Comanche, a crime which caused a reward to be offered for him dead or alive. Hardin disappeared from Texas, but John Armstrong heard he was in Florida, and he got permission to go after him. Armstrong learned that Hardin and some companions were coming to Pensacola on a train. The officers boarded the train at a small station, and, as Armstrong entered the car with a long-barreled six-shooter in his hand, Hardin recognized it as a favorite Texas weapon. Hardin reached for his gun, but it hung on his suspenders, giving Armstrong time to kill his companion and club Hardin into submission. He sent General Steele this telegram:

ARRESTED JOHN WESLEY HARDIN PENSACOLA, FLORIDA, THIS P.M. HE HAD FOUR MEN WITH HIM. ONE OF THEIR NUMBER KILLED, ALL THE REST CAPTURED. . . .

Hardin was captured August 23, 1877, and was guarded by Captain N. O. Reynolds' company of Rangers until he was tried in September and sentenced to the penitentiary. One of the Ranger guards, who had a flair for writing, gave this report from the Comanche jail:

"Day before yesterday Lieut. Reynolds, commanding Company E of the Frontier Battalion, arrived at this place guarding John Wesley Hardin. . . . Hardin deported himself with the utmost decorum. . . . He is what the ladies would call a blond; about five feet ten inches high; and is fairly educated. . . . He is confined in the jail at this place, heavily sealed on the inside with oak, containing an iron cage. He is also ironed and guarded by Rangers, who remain within the prison wall both day and night."

Hardin was sentenced to twenty-five years in the penitentiary, pardoned in 1893, and then killed by John Selman in El Paso in 1895. His companion, King Fisher, along with another Texas gunman, Ben Thompson, was killed in the Vaudeville Theater in San Antonio, March 11, 1884. The bad men were being thinned out in Texas, by the Rangers, by one another. Many names had been crossed off in the well-thumbed Book of Wanted Men.

CHAPTER XVI

THE SALT WAR AT EL PASO

STARTING a war is like starting a fire. You have to have kindling and tinder. A war starts in a small way, with a small act. It is easily stamped out, but soon gets out of control, and is terribly destructive. The Salt War was waged around El Paso in the last weeks of 1877. At that time El Paso lay four or five hundred miles west of the line of settlement in central Texas. Around it, partly in Texas and partly in Mexico, lived about 12,000 Mexicans and 80 Americans.

The Mexicans had lived there for a long time, tilling their little fields and raising a few cattle, sheep, and goats. They were ordinarily a peaceful lot, but were ignorant, suspicious of strangers, and easily misled.

They did not trust the Americans, and for this we cannot blame them. The Americans had defeated their nation in war, taken their territory, and made them foreigners in the land of their birth. They came like conquerors, speaking a different language, supporting a different law, believing in a different religion in so far as they believed in any at all. These bold, swaggering Americans took the political offices, controlled the courts, and ignored the Mexicans except at election time.

To call these eighty English-speaking people Americans is to speak loosely. They were of all nationalities—a German named Schutze; a Frenchman named Fountain; two Italians; Cardis, the polished gentleman; and Borajo, the evil priest. There were Atkinson, McBride, and Magoffin—who might have been anything—and Charles Howard— strong, domineering, and greedy. These men the Mexicans could not trust. Some were greedy for money, some for votes—all were greedy for salt.

[95]

Salt, so common now, has not always been plentiful. Its rare occurrence inland, and the fact that both man and beast must have it, led kings to monopolize it and lay a tax on it. The Americans in El Paso undertook to imitate the kings, and the Salt War resulted.

The salt bed lies about 110 miles east of El Paso on the Texas side of the Rio Grande. For more than a century the Mexicans—and the Spaniards before them—had gone there to get salt. Nobody objected when the Mexicans yoked their oxen to high-wheeled carts and set out on the long journey. The salt was free, and the Mexicans came from both sides of the river for it.

Some of the Americans decided to acquire the salt beds and charge the Mexicans for taking it. These men were known as the Salt Ring. In this ring were Luis Cardis; the priest, Antonio Borajo; and the Italians.

A. J. Fountain ran for the Senate, promising the Mexicans that if they would elect him he would obtain the salt lakes for the people. The Mexicans elected him, making him leader of the Anti-Salt Ring.

The members of both rings were Republicans, as were most of the Americans. Now the Republican party was split over salt, and there was danger that the Democrats would take over, as they had done in the rest of the state. To avert such disaster, the two factions came together to make a compromise. No compromise could be reached on account of the priest. Borajo demanded control of the public schools and their teachers. He wanted Fountain to take the salt lakes in his own name. Borajo would then advise the Mexicans to pay for the salt, and Fountain would divide the proceeds with the priest. Luis Cardis did not go along with the plan, remarking that the priest had "salt on the brain," thought there was a fortune in it, and that no one could enjoy the salt without coming to terms with Borajo. Fountain had the decency to refuse Borajo's demands, and the split in the Republican party was made permanent.

Into this gap walked Charles Howard, the Democrat, more selfish but less cunning than the Republicans. He became a partner with Cardis and Borajo, and as a boss of the Mexican votes took the salt in his own name and agreed to divide the money as suggested. Immediately the crooks fell out. Howard set out to survey the salt lakes, notifying the Mexicans that they would henceforth have to pay him for the salt. On the way to the salt lakes he stopped at the Quitman stage station, owned by Cardis. Here Howard attacked Cardis, who was not a fighting man. Cardis escaped by running under a table; Howard remarked that he was too cowardly to kill.

When the Mexicans heard what Howard had done, they organized a mob. They captured Howard and made him give up claim to the salt lakes and agree to leave El Paso forever. Howard signed the papers in a storm and was conducted through the angry mob by Father Pierre Bourgade, as good a priest as Borajo was evil.

If Cardis figured that he could get rid of his enemy by banishment, he left out of account the nature of the man. Howard was already on his way back from Mesilla, New Mexico. On October 7, Cardis wrote in his diary: "Captain Courtney advised me to be on the lookout, for Howard is making desperate threats of my life."

Three days later, Cardis was in Schutze's store dictating a letter when Howard entered with a double-barreled shotgun. Cardis rose and moved behind a high desk with only his legs visible. Howard emptied one barrel of the gun into Cardis' legs, and as the body sank down, fired the other barrel into it. He reloaded the gun, walked slowly from the room, and returned to New Mexico.

The death of their champion, Cardis, infuriated the Mexicans and they unleashed their fury on Howard's friends and bondsmen. More and more Mexicans from across the Rio Grande drifted over and joined the mob, which now had virtual possession of the county.

News of the trouble went to Austin. It would take thirty days for a Ranger company to reach El Paso. General Steele ordered Major Jones to go alone to see what he could do to prevent further trouble.

When Major Jones arrived, the mob had Howard's bondsmen surrounded at San Elizario. Major Jones could get no help. The army officers refused to interfere, the Mexicans were unreliable, and there were not enough decent Americans to form a posse. Major Jones went out to the mob, accompanied by Father Pierre Bourgade, and together this man of the state and the man of the church worked to restore order. Major Jones told the Mexicans that he could not settle the salt question, that the courts would have to do that. His business was to keep the peace. Though the Mexicans agreed to keep the peace, Father Bourgade heard them murmur and was fearful that violence lay ahead.

Lacking a trusted and experienced Ranger, Major Jones selected John B. Tays, made him a lieutenant in Company C, and gathered such men as he could find to serve with him. Then he went to Mesilla, New Mexico, and brought Howard to El Paso and put him under bond. Major Jones left El Paso on November 22, hoping that Tays would prove competent and that Howard would not return to El Paso.

Howard might have remained away had the Mexicans left the salt alone. Early in December sixteen carts and wagons set out for the salt lakes. Howard heard of this and preferred charges against them. By December 12 and 13, Howard had returned to El Paso, and in the company of four Rangers went to the Ranger camp at San Elizario. The mob formed under the leadership of Chico Barela, surrounded the camp, and put it under siege.

The siege lasted three days; the mob grew larger and drew its lines tighter around the camp. At the end of two days the Mexicans asked for a truce, and in the darkness tunneled under the buildings to plant dynamite. They now told the Americans that, unless Howard would come down of his own will and surrender, they would blow up the whole place. It was not possible to escape the mob. One man, Ellis, attempted to go through the lines, but two days later was brought back in a gunny sack, scalped, his throat cut, stabbed twice in the heart.

[98]

Another, Andrew Loomis, was captured. The mob was determined to have Howard at all costs.

When the mob demanded him, Howard knew his death warrant had been signed. In spite of his greed and unyielding nature, he showed courage. "I will go," he said, "as it is the only way to save your lives, but they will kill me." He gave his personal belongings to John McBride, told his friends good-by, and went out with Lieutenant Tays to the mob. The mob now sent for Atkinson to interpret, and soon sent him back with orders from Tays for the Rangers and other men to come down with their arms, that all would be arranged peaceably. All the Americans were promptly disarmed, and now the mob had everything in its own hands.

Chico Barela, the leader, may have intended to act in good faith, but the mob was in a frenzy and demanded blood. The question was: How much blood? Who should die? Certainly Howard, but what of his bondsman, Atkinson and his agent, McBride? Barela might have saved these two had it not been for Borajo. "Shoot all the gringos and I will absolve you," he said, but Barela would not go that far. Three were selected.

Howard was the most important, and the first chosen for the firing squad. His hands were not bound, and as he walked erect to the place designated by his executioners, silence spread over the wide land. In broken Spanish he told the Mexicans that their act would cost the lives of three hundred men. He faced the guns, struck his breast, and said *"Fire."* The rifles belched smoke and punctured the stillness. Howard fell, writhed in death, and an excited Mexican, Jesus Telles, ran up and struck at the body with his *machete,* missed, and cut off two of his own toes.

McBride came next, and was killed instantly.

Then came Atkinson, who spoke Spanish. He reminded the Mexicans of their pledge, and asked them if they were going to break the word that had been given. But the mob was beyond reason, and cried out *"Acabenlos!"* meaning "Finish them!"

"Then there is no remedy?" he asked.

"No, no!" shouted the mob.

Atkinson removed his coat and opened his shirt to lay bare his breast, indicating where the guns should be aimed.

[99]

"I will give the word," he told the Mexicans.

He faced the guns and said, "When I give the word, fire at my heart." Then, so that all could hear, he spoke the one word, *"Fire."*

Five bullets struck him—in the belly. He staggered but did not fall, and cried out in Spanish, "Higher up, you *cabrones*." Two more shots were fired, and he fell but was not dead. He motioned to his head, and a Mexican shot him at close range with a pistol.

The mob howled and danced with glee. Its members, now turned into a plundering band, ransacked the houses in San Elizario and cried out for the blood of the Rangers and the other Americans. Chico Barela, the leader, told the mob that they had done enough, and that if another man was harmed he would turn the guns of his men on them. The Rangers and others were freed the next day. They rode back into El Paso minus their arms, December 18, 1877.

The Americans rearmed, got recruits from New Mexico and any place else where fighting men could be found. A motley band composed of Tays' Rangers, Sheriff Kerber's posse, and an assortment of gunmen recruited from New Mexico set out for San Elizario on December 22. They loaded coffins on a wagon in which to bury Howard and his companions, and left with two prisoners sitting on the coffins. They killed the prisoners.

At Socorro they surrounded a house, killed the man, wounded a woman, and reported that they did it because they were fired on. In this village lived Jesus Telles, who had cut off his two toes when striking at the wounded Howard. He was killed by the Rangers. Before the Rangers and posse reached San Elizario, General Edward Hatch warned them that the road ahead was lined with armed men and advised them to go no further. They returned to Ysleta to pass the Christmas holidays.

It was not until December 28 that the party reached the place where the Americans had died. The bodies had been dragged from the place of execution and thrown in a well. The mob had taken all the dead men's clothing except Howard's socks and shirt. Howard's body had been mutilated. Atkinson and McBride were buried in San Elizario, but Howard's body was returned to El Paso, known then as Franklin. The mob had melted, as it were, into the desert. The Mexicans had scat-

[101]

tered to their homes, or fled from them to secret places. The Salt War, which nobody won, was over. The fire had burned itself out.

The President of the United States took notice of it because of its international character. Three men were appointed to make an investigation. President Rutherford B. Hayes appointed two army officers, and Governor Hubbard appointed Major John B. Jones as a third member. This board met at Fort Bliss on January 16, 1878, and made its report on March 16. Estimates of property damaged ranged from $12,-000 to more than $30,000. There was no estimate as to the loss of human life. If any person was legally punished for the various crimes committed in the Salt War, there is no record of it.

Had Major Jones been able to stay in El Paso, he probably could have averted the disaster. A company of experienced Rangers under a competent officer could have handled the crisis. The appointment of Tays and of the men who served under him was a makeshift business that did not work. Neither Tays nor any of his men had the stuff out of which a Texas Ranger is made. There is not in the long history of the force any other case where a Texas Ranger surrendered. In doing so, Tays broke a long and honorable record and left the darkest blot on the history of the force.

CHAPTER XVII

THE LAW AND THE OUTLAW AT ROUND ROCK

N February 18, 1878, Major Jones arrived in El Paso to serve as one of the commissioners appointed by the president and the governor to make a final report on the Salt War. Four days later, February 22, Washington's birthday, Sam Bass robbed his first train in Texas at Allen Station near Dallas. On March 16, Major Jones signed the Salt War report, and two days later Sam robbed another train at Hutchins, also near Dallas. He made it four in a row by holding up a third train at Eagle Ford on April 4, and a fourth one at Mesquite on April 14. In fifty days he became the champion train robber of Texas.

Ten days after the last holdup, Major Jones went to Dallas to take charge of the frantic hunt for the most wanted man in the state. It took him three months plus one week to find Sam Bass, just eighteen miles from Austin in the little town of Round Rock.

A bandit and train robber is not made overnight. He starts in a small way. Since there are no schools where banditry is taught, the outlaw's instruction is irregular, given by circumstances and associates.

Sam Bass was a country boy, born July 21, 1851, near Mitchell, Indiana. His mother died when he was ten, his father when he was about thirteen, and these unfortunate events probably had much to do with Sam's future. He and his brothers and sisters were sent to live with an uncle on a farm. Sam remained with his uncle about five years. He went to school a little, but was not a bright scholar. He barely learned to read and never to write. Nor did he especially like to work. He and his uncle had a quarrel, and Sam left this home never to return. Much of what has been told is in the first stanza of the Sam Bass Ballad, a part of the Texas folklore:

Sam Bass was born in Indiana, it was his native home
And at the age of seventeen, young Sam began to roam;
He first came out to Texas, a teamster for to be.
A kinder-hearted fellow you scarcely ever see.

Sam went first to St. Louis, then down the great river to Rosedale, Mississippi, where he worked in a sawmill, improved his game of poker, and saved enough money to take him to the land of his dreams.

Sam left for Texas in the summer of 1870, traveling with a family named Mayes. He arrived in the fall, got a job on a ranch, but did not make a good cowboy. He was not a good rider or shot, foremen would not take him on the cattle drives to Kansas, and the buffalo hunters wanted more experienced men. As for fighting Indians, that was risky business for a greenhorn. Sam was employed by Sheriff W. F. Eagan of Denton, not as a deputy who could carry a gun, but more as a hired hand who curried the horses, milked the cows, cut firewood, and built fences. For a time he drove a freight wagon between Dallas and Denton. He got acquainted with the country and came to know all the trails and roads and thickets which he used when he turned bandit.

His circle of friends widened, and came to include many of his later partners in crime. There was Jim Murphy, the saloon keeper's son; Frank Jackson, who worked in a tin shop; Henry Underwood, the wood-hauler and freighter; and the Collins boys, Joel, Billy, and Henry. These were rowdy young men who liked nothing better than to run horse races outside the town on Sunday afternoons. Sam loved the horses, and nothing thrilled him as much as to see them coming down the track with riders whipping and spurring.

He fell in love with a little chestnut sorrel mare of Steel Dust stock, acquired her, and found that he had the fastest horse in that part of Texas.

Sam used to deal in race stock,
One called the Denton mare.
He matched her in scrub races
And took her to the fair.

Sam now struck out on his own and went to the wild bunch. The mare won so many races in north Texas that Sam had difficulty in getting bets. In 1875 he and two companions went three hundred miles south, to San Antonio. There they met Joel Collins, who became their leader and an evil influence. Joel had had much experience, had killed a man, and gone three times up the Chisholm trail to Kansas. Bass sold the Denton mare and went in with Collins to gather a herd of cattle for the northern trail. They gathered seven hundred head of longhorns on credit, to be paid for after the cattle were delivered. They sold the cattle, paid off the hands, pocketed the money, and set off for the Black Hills of South Dakota where gold had been discovered. They lost the money in gambling and speculation and then turned to robbing stages, but had poor luck. Suspicion soon fell on them, they became "too hot," and then set off across the plains towards Texas.

THE ROBBERY OF TRAIN NO. 4

On their way south they had to cross the Union Pacific tracks over which big trains thundered between California and St. Louis. Surely there would be a great deal of money on those trains, carried in the express car or by well-heeled passengers. Joel Collins was still the leader, and he had five men to help him—Bill Heffridge, Jim Berry, Tom Nixon, Jack Davis, and Sam Bass. This gang decided to strike the eastbound passenger train at Big Springs, Nebraska. It was a small place where there would be few people. The train came through at 10:48 at night; the robbers would have long hours of darkness before daylight would reveal their trail. The date selected was September 18, 1877.

The robbery of train No. 4 went off on schedule. The gang took about thirteen hundred dollars from the passengers, but made the big strike in the express car, where they found three wooden boxes each containing $20,000 of bright new twenty-dollar gold pieces from the San Francisco mint. This was the payoff, and each of the six robbers had a little more than $10,000 in cash, besides several good gold watches and other items taken from passengers.

The six train robbers divided into three pairs, each pair taking their part of the loot. Collins and Heffridge turned southeast, bound for San Antonio, Berry and Nixon went to Kansas City, while Jack Davis and Sam Bass chose another route, heading for Denton, Texas. Just one week from the date of the robbery, September 25, 1877, Joel Collins and Bill Heffridge were killed by a sheriff's posse and some soldiers at

Buffalo Station, sixty miles west of Big Springs. They had $20,000 on a pack pony.

On October 14, less than a month after the robbery, Jim Berry was shot by a posse at Mexico, Missouri, and died two days later. His partner, Nixon, caught a train to Chicago and was later reported to have gone to Canada. Bass and Davis, disguised as farmers and cowboys, had arrived in Denton County on November 1. Davis caught a train to New Orleans and was not heard from any more.

When Sam Bass showed up in Denton, his name had not been connected with the robbery of the Union Pacific; he explained his prosperity by vague tales of having struck it rich in the gold mines.

If Sam was disturbed by the fact that three of his companions of the U. P. robbery had been killed by officers of the law, and that the other two had fled into complete oblivion, he gave no indication of it. He had never had so much money or so many friends of the wrong kind. It is true that he stayed in the brush, coming into Denton at night. He gradually brought into his camp Frank Jackson, Seaborn Barnes, Henry Underwood, Arkansas Johnson, Tom Spotswood, and Jim Murphy.

Sam was a free spender, and the U. P. gold went fast. By the spring of 1878 it must have been running out. Then it was that he organized his gang and began robbing Texas trains. He made four strikes in less than sixty days. He used from four to seven men, struck in the early part of the night so that he could get away in the darkness, and usually retreated to the creek bottoms of Denton County. Arkansas Johnson was killed in a fight on Salt Creek, July 13, 1878, by Captain June Peak's Texas Rangers.

When Major Jones entered the Sam Bass hunt at Dallas on April 14, four days after the last train robbery, he found the whole country in turmoil. By this time it was known that Sam Bass was leading the robbers. but nobody could find Sam in the dense thickets of Denton County.

Major Jones selected June Peak, who had been with McNelly in the Civil War, made him first a lieutenant and then a captain, and told Peak to follow the robbers until he caught them or ran them out of the country.

After Peak's Rangers had killed Arkansas Johnson and captured the bandits' horses, Bass learned that Henry Underwood, Charley Carter, and Henry Collins—Joel's brother—had quit him. He had left only Seaborn Barnes and Frank Jackson.

North Texas was getting too hot for them, and they decided to leave that part of the country. In the meantime, however, they were joined by Jim Murphy, who had been in jail in Tyler. When Major Jones entered the hunt, he began to look for the weak link in the bandit chain —informers, men who would talk. He knew who the train robbers were and had all their names and descriptions; he also knew those who befriended them and helped them, or had knowledge of their plans. He began to arrest all these people and to put them in jail. The Murphy family had been friendly to Sam Bass. They had fed him, changed his money, and warned him when danger was near. Major Jones had Henderson Murphy, the saloon keeper, and his two sons jailed for harboring the outlaws. It was getting dangerous even to know Sam Bass.

Jim Murphy proved to be the weak link. At Tyler Major Jones learned that Murphy was ready "to give poor Sam away," and he went to see him to perfect a plan that would put an end to the bandit panic. Murphy said that if the Rangers would set him free, he would join Sam Bass and inform the Rangers where the robbers could be found. Major Jones allowed Murphy to go free; Murphy agreed to join Bass and keep the Rangers informed as to the plans of the outlaws. Thus it was that Jim Murphy showed up in the Bass camp on June 15, just as Sam, Frank Jackson, and Seaborn Barnes had decided to leave the dangerous Denton-Dallas country.

Before the party finally left, word that Jim Murphy was a spy was brought to the ears of Bass and his men. They held a council of war. Barnes and Bass wanted to kill Murphy, but Jackson saved his life. But the suspicion had been raised. Murphy was watched all the time by Barnes and Bass and found it extremely difficult to get free of them to mail letters to Major Jones.

The four men rode south and finally reached Waco, a hundred miles from Dallas. By this time they had decided to rob a bank, a place where they were sure to find money, more than they had found in four train robberies. They looked over a bank in Waco, but Murphy persuaded them that it was a bad risk, stalling for time until he could notify Major Jones. They finally decided to rob the bank at Round Rock, and at Belton Murphy managed to send a letter with this intelligence to Major Jones at Austin. The men camped in the brush north of the village, rested their horses, and got a Negro woman, Mary Matson, to cook them some biscuits. When opportunity presented they would ride into the village to look the bank over and to make plans. They needed money, for Sam changed his last twenty-dollar gold piece in a saloon at Belton.

When Major Jones heard that Round Rock had been chosen, he began to concentrate men there to await the bandits. The Rangers did not know when the strike would come, or that Bass had decided to hit the bank on Saturday, July 20, but the men were there and ready a day before, on a Friday.

Bass on his part thought it would be a good idea to ride in on Friday and take a final look. All four men rode out of the brush, but Jim Murphy was nervous, and on some excuse dropped out of the party at a store in Old Round Rock. It was Bass, Barnes, and Frank Jackson who went on into the new village that had grown up near the railway station. They hitched their horses in an alley and went into a store to buy some tobacco from a clerk named Simon Jude.

Two deputy sheriffs, A. W. Grimes and Maurice Moore, had come to Round Rock with Major Jones. They saw the three strangers who looked like cowboys go by and decided that one of them had a pistol. The officers followed them into the store and asked one of the strangers if he had a pistol. Then the shooting started. Grimes fell dead outside the door and Moore was wounded, as was one of the strangers, probably Bass. At the sound of the shooting, the Texas Rangers came from their hiding, among them George Harrell and Dick Ware. The street of the sleepy town was soon full of sound and pistol smoke. The strangers ran for their horses, firing as they went. Major Jones was coming from the depot where he had gone to send a telegram, and so far as can be learned fired the only shot in his long service as leader of the Frontier Battalion.

About the time the three men reached their horses in the alley, Seaborn Barnes was killed and Bass fatally wounded. Frank Jackson helped Bass on his horse, mounted his own, and they escaped towards Old Round Rock. They passed Jim Murphy, who was still at the store. Murphy said that Sam was very pale, barely able to cling to his horse. In a short time Major Jones and the other officers came riding in hot pursuit, but the robbers had disappeared.

The next day, the Rangers found Sam Bass under a tree not far from where the outlaws had camped. Frank Jackson had bound up his wounds as best he could, and then ridden off never to be heard from. They brought Bass into town, got Dr. Cockran to tend his wounds, but very little could be done for him. He died on Sunday, July 21, 1878, his twenty-seventh birthday. Thus it is when the law meets the outlaw, and thus will it ever be. There were some later train robberies in Texas, but no man matched the record made by the boy from Indiana. The mind of Major Jones was too much for the morals of Sam Bass. Sam's career had been brief. It was just ten months and three days from the time of the U. P. robbery to the date of his death. In the ten months he had robbed five trains.

Major Jones's appointment with Sam Bass marks almost the end of his career in the field. In 1879 he was made adjutant general, and his duties required him to remain in Austin. His hard service had affected his health. He died July 19, 1881, three years from the day of his meeting with Sam Bass in Round Rock. The Frontier Battalion which he organized and led with such distinction was not the same after his death. An end had come to an era. But before leaving this romantic period of Ranger history, let us take a closer look at the life of the Ranger.

CHAPTER XVIII

LIFE IN THE TEXAS RANGERS

T HE way the Texas Ranger lived can be understood only by looking at the kind of work he did, and the conditions under which he did it. Though a Ranger was a fighting man, his was not a military order. Since his business was that of protecting the citizens from their enemies, he was like a peace officer, but he was not a policeman in the ordinary sense any more than he was a soldier. The force held a place somewhere between that of an army and a police force. When he was going to meet an outside enemy—Indians or Mexicans —he was pretty close to being a soldier. When he had to turn to enemies from within his own society—outlaws, train robbers, highwaymen and thieves—he was more the detective and policeman.

The Rangers were organized into companies like soldiers, but not into regiments or brigades. They were too few for that. The company was in the charge of a captain or a lieutenant and might have a sergeant. The headquarters was in Austin, the capital, and the captains reported to the headquarters officer; under the Republic this was the secretary of war and under the state it was until 1935 the adjutant general.

The Rangers differed from soldiers in many ways. As already stated, they never wore uniform, they never engaged in military drill, they had no flag, they never saluted an officer. They had no regular barracks and garrisoned no forts. They did have camps, but they moved them often. The relation between the captain and his Rangers was somewhat like that between a sheriff and his deputies.

The Rangers differed from a city police force, whose members also wear uniforms and engage in formal drill. The main difference between a Ranger and a police officer or sheriff is that the Ranger operates over the entire state, can go anywhere that duty calls within the state, while the policeman is limited by the city boundaries, and the sheriff and the deputies by the county boundaries. The word Ranger suggests one who ranges—over a wide territory—in this case all of Texas. The Ranger was like a police officer in that he could arrest citizens, something the soldier cannot ordinarily do. The police officer can make arrests within the city limits, the sheriff and his deputies within the county limits, the Ranger anywhere within the state limits. The city policeman has a beat a mile or five miles long, the sheriff has one of thirty miles, but the Texas Rangers have a beat of five hundred to a thousand miles.

Since the Rangers were few and their territory big, they could not afford to deal with petty law-breakers. The Ranger was called in when the task got too big for the local officers, when the outlaw of whatever kind could not be caught or controlled by the city or county officers. He was called in before conditions got to such a state as to require martial law, the help of the army itself.

Because the Ranger had such a long beat to patrol, it follows that he had to travel a great deal. This made transportation a big item in his life, and in the early days the horse was the best—in fact, the only—form of transportation that he could use. The Ranger loved his horse, made him a companion, and cared for him first.

REQUIREMENTS FOR A RANGER

The captain was the most important man in the Ranger company. Though a Ranger would often go alone to the scene of trouble, he always returned to the captain to report what he had done. The captain was his headquarters when he was in the field. He had the right to choose his own men, and on his judgment the character of the company depended. Captain Tom Hickman remarked that a Ranger's examination consisted of three questions: Can you shoot? Can you ride? Can you cook? If the answer was yes to these three questions, the applicant had at least got by the first barrier. Actually, there was more to it than this. The Ranger had to have youth, a durable body, and an up-bringing that would be useful to him in the arduous work. A boy who had grown up in the country was a better prospect than a city boy. A boy who had grown up on a cattle ranch, who knew how to find his way about on the open range, who knew how to ride a horse and how to take care of him was more likely to make a good Ranger than one who had grown up on a farm.

The Texas Ranger furnished his own horse and arms. As already stated, the horse had to be a good one, and the captain inspected the horse as carefully as he did the man. The horse needed speed for use in emergencies, and he needed what the Westerner calls "bottom." This means endurance, the ability to travel for many days carrying the man and his baggage. It was necessary for the horse to live on grass. The best horses for this service were those with a strain of mustang or Spanish blood, with a mixture of the cultivated breeds, such as the thoroughbred. There was no tougher horse than the Spanish mustang, and none in America as hardy, as able to live on grass and to go long periods without water. The Ranger, unlike the cowboy, did not have a "string" of horses; he had only one, and it therefore had to be the best.

The cowboy and the Ranger were closely kin, alike in their attitude

and in their equipment. They lived in the same country, both lived in the open, each knew how to depend on himself, how to cook, ride, and shoot. The cowboy rode after cattle and horses; the Ranger rode after bad men; and both rode well. Since they both rode much of the time, their clothes were similar, suited to a horseman. Though the Ranger had no prescribed uniform, he did in general wear clothes and carry equipment that set him apart. His clothes were horse-clothes and his equipment was that of a fighting man. This combination, together with his background, has led to the quip that a Texas Ranger was a cowboy with a commission.

In describing the Ranger's clothes we can start with either his head or feet, because he took more pride in his headgear and footgear than in any other part of his dress. His hat was of the best quality, and this was necessary because he put it to many uses. In the later period it was always a Stetson, with high crown and fairly broad brim. It takes a good hat to stick on a man's head when he is riding a spirited horse. The brim must be flexible, but not floppy. The Ranger did not want his vision

cut off by having a hatbrim over his eyes on a running horse in a high wind. He used his hat as a drinking cup when he came to water, for signaling, and to shade his face when he was taking a nap under a tree at midday.

The boots were shop-made and more expensive than the hat. They had pointed toes, high heels, and were often decorated with inlay and stitched design. In the early days the boot fitted snug to the leg, and came almost to the bend of the knee. The modern boot has a shorter leg, half knee-length, and is bigger so that the wearer can stuff his trousers in it. The boot looks out of place in the city, but it was designed for a horseman, for the man—cowboy or Texas Ranger—who works on horseback. It is the most comfortable and useful footgear ever invented for such workmen. It was not intended for Saturday-evening cowboys or drug-store sheriffs.

What went in between the hat and the boots was not important to the Ranger. It might be a wool or cotton shirt, and blue jeans trousers. But one rule had to be observed. There could be nothing floppy that would get in the way of the free use of the arms, that would frighten a horse, that would hinder the use of rope, knife, reins, or revolver. The Ranger had to be ready to run, rope, shoot, or quit a falling horse. He never wore suspenders, but always a belt of the best leather, often with an expensive silver buckle. He had no use for the ordinary coat, but wore what was called a round-a-bout—a short jacket, something like a vest, which fitted close to his body, leaving his gun exposed on his hip.

The Ranger used the Western or cowboy saddle. He could not abide the military or Virginia saddle, which in his opinion made a man look like "a frog on a shovel." He rode western style, as a part of the horse,

the way the Spaniards, the Arabs, and real horsemen everywhere have ridden. Throughout Texas there were—and still are—saddlemakers as well as bootmakers—and they are often the same, catering to the need of men who live on horseback.

This heavy western saddle had ample skirts to house the middle part of the horse and keep him well separated from all parts of the rider. This saddle had a high fork and a horn for roping cattle; it had a high cantle, which when combined with a swell-fork, gave the rider a firm seat. The saddle is fitted with many strings, front and rear. There is a horn string to carry a coiled rope or to hang the saddle when it is not in use. Pairs of strings are to the front, and pairs to the rear of the rider. To these are attached a slicker, an extra blanket, and such other gear as the rider may need. This western saddle is a modification of that used by the Mexicans, who borrowed it from the Spaniards, who borrowed it from the Moors, who borrowed it from the Arabs so long ago that no one knows who originated it.

The bridle is also western. The unruly mustang horses used in Texas could be managed only by a severe bit. This was often inlaid with silver, and of the finest steel. The headstall was made of the best leather.

The blanket was expensive, a real Navajo if it could be obtained, one that served many purposes. It was fitted under the saddle to protect the horse during the long rides, and at night it was both over and under the Ranger to protect him from the ground below and the cold above.

THE RANGER'S ARMS

Since the Texas Ranger was a fighting man, his arms were of major importance. When the force was formed in 1835, the firearms were still primitive, cap-and-ball rifle which had developed in Kentucky and Pennsylvania and the horse pistol. Such weapons are now found in curio

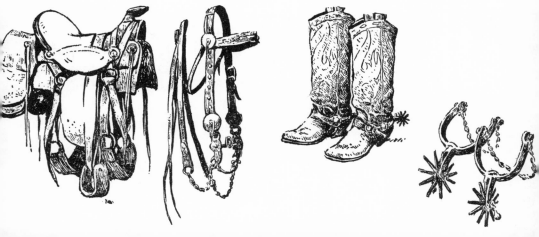

shops and museums. In the early fights with the Indians the Rangers found that they needed a weapon that carried more than one shot, and that could be used on horseback. This need was supplied by Samuel Colt, as told in Chapter V. The Ranger carried his revolver in a scabbard attached to his belt. There are two ways of carrying the revolver. If worn on the right hip, the stock or grip points to the rear so that the Ranger's hand rests naturally on it. Some carry the revolver on the left hip, stock pointing forward, so that the wearer reaches across his own body to draw the weapon. There is a good deal of talk about men who carried two guns, one on each hip. This is mostly talk, and it is quite certain that more of these two-gun men have been seen in the movies than in all Texas or western history. Two-gun men were very few, and extremely scarce among Texas Rangers.

The Ranger also had the best rifle obtainable. In the later years this was likely to be a Winchester or a Remington, but in the early years, prior to 1860, there were practically no cartridge guns, and certainly no magazine guns. The rifle was carried in a long scabbard under the left leg of the rider with the barrel pointed downward and to the rear.

The Ranger carried one or more pairs of handcuffs, and he might even have leg-irons for use on very bad characters.

In the early period such camp equipment as a Ranger company might have was moved on pack-mules, rather than in wagons such as were used in ranch work. Hays' regiment of Texas Rangers who served in the Mexican War were not even given tents, but camped in the open or under such shelter as they could get. Cooking was done on an open fire, either with Dutch ovens or without them. The Rangers contrived to have coffee and flour, usually beans, but for meat they often depended mainly on the game they killed. There is no record that they used the chuckwagon, and so they must have carried all their camp plunder on pack-mules or on their own horses. The Rangers had no regular cooks. Every man in an outfit was supposed to be able to cook, and each man was supposed to take his turn at the camp task. In the later period, especially in Major Jones' Frontier Battalion, camps were set up along the western frontier with equipment—pots, pans, Dutch ovens, axes, and tents, rather luxurious when compared to the earlier days.

In moving across country, a company of Rangers traveled mainly in the daytime, usually sticking to the divides rather than to the established routes. They knew that practically all streams in Texas have a southeast course, and they seemed to be able to make their way without getting lost. They tried to camp on a stream, or by a waterhole. If they approached a stream, they would cross it before making camp to safeguard against a rise which might cut them off. They would picket their horses on stake ropes, or hobble them so that they could not wander far. The horses were trained to manage rope and hobbles, and would not injure themselves. The Comanches and Apaches liked nothing better than to slip into a Ranger camp, cut the ropes, and run off the horses. It was said that a Ranger on foot was no Ranger at all, that a Ranger was no better than his horse. To prevent losing horses, the Rangers in Indian country would put out night guards, but one or two men traveling alone would let the horse graze on a rope with the loose end tied to the sleeping Rangers' wrist.

In traveling, the Texas Ranger was welcome in all the homes in the

towns and villages. He was looked upon as a protector and a friend, the man who could stand off the Indians or any other raiders of the settlement. In the villages and towns, he would head for the office of the sheriff or other peace officer. He could always find a bed at the sheriff's office, in the jail. From such men he obtained information, and to them he gave information. There was no better place to gather news, to learn what was going on, than in the saloons and bars. It was here that the criminal element or representatives and informers could be found, and the Ranger was always on the lookout for them.

SPORTS THE RANGERS PLAYED

Amusements of the Rangers were usually related to their work. They liked to attend horse races, and would occasionally engage in them. In San Antonio and south along the border the Mexican settlers had many games played on horseback. In one of these games a chicken was the prize, with two groups of mounted contestants. One rider took the chicken and set off for his opponent's goal. The other riders tried to block him, to ride him down, or take the chicken from him. It was a rough game, hard on horses, dangerous to men, and fatal to the chicken.

The Mexicans loved cockfights, and still do, and there is evidence that the Rangers attended these games and took chances on them. It was said of Jack Hays that he would "heel a chicken."

Another horse sport that Rangers played at was the tournament. In this game small rings are suspended in a row from posts. The player, using a pointed stick, a lance, rides at a fast pace down the path, and catches as many rings as possible on his lance. The winner of the tournament was rewarded with a wreath, and this he presented to the girl of his choice, making her queen of the tournament.

Shooting matches were common, and many of the frontiersmen were uncommon marksmen. The Ranger was expected to be an excellent marksman, an expert in handling any weapon. There was nothing he liked better than "rolling a can"—that is, keeping it on the move with four or five shots fired from his pistol in rapid succession. He liked to practice the quick draw, and it was necessary for him to know how to draw and fire quickly. The pistol lacks the accuracy of a rifle, and the experienced pistol marksman does not actually use the sights as a rifleman does. He learns that he can use a pistol almost as he does a finger. He has no trouble in pointing his finger at a target, and he learns to "point" the pistol in the same way.

Rifle shooting is another matter. The rifle must be aimed. The gunman must "catch the sights." In shooting matches the target might be an ace of spades on a tree, it might be a nail set so that the bullet would sink it in the tree, it might be a wand the size of an arrow shaft, or a silver dime that some spendthrift was willing to risk. The most difficult target was that used in the turkey shoot. The turkey was tied behind a log so that nothing but his head could be seen. A turkey keeps his head in constant motion, bobbing up and down, or turning from side to side. There was only a split-second when a bullet could find the turkey's head where it was when the hammer fell. The turkey was the prize for the man who shot off its head.

The question is often asked as to what became of the Rangers when they quit being Rangers. Their work as peace officers, and their reputation, created a demand for them in civil and political life. It was not difficult for an ex-Ranger to be elected sheriff of his own country, especially if the country had a tough and lawless element that had defied previous officers. Others became deputies. Some became county judges; one became governor. It must be remembered that most of them were young, and few men wanted to make a career of the rough wandering life that a Ranger had to lead. Their travels over Texas put them in contact with important men, and gave them an opportunity to locate land suited to their taste. Many Rangers became ranchmen.

This glimpse of Ranger life leaves the question unanswered as to why these men were so effective. They were few in number, and were assigned the toughest job. The answer is that they were selected in a hard and rugged school. Many were called but few were chosen. They had youth, strength, and endurance. They all had courage. The individual was powerful because he was clothed with the authority of the state. He was conscious of this authority, and he knew how to act with decision. He knew how to protect himself, and how to take his opponent off guard. The Ranger was a master of the unexpected. He was effective because he knew two things: when to strike and how to strike with such speed and accuracy as to demoralize or destroy his enemy.

CHAPTER XIX

COPS AND ROBBERS: FENCE CUTTERS AND PRIZE-FIGHTERS

THE last decades of the nineteenth century brought a change in Ranger activity. The biggest jobs of the previous decades had been done: the Indians driven out, feuds quieted, mobs quelled, and the bank robbers laid in their graves.

During the next twenty years the Rangers played a cop-and-robber game wherever they were needed in the state. Some of the more stirring episodes of this period are related in this chapter.

In 1873 barbed wire was invented, and by 1880 the open ranges of Texas were being converted into fenced pastures and farms. "Don't fence me in" was the cry of those who liked free grass and the open range. For ten years—1880–1890—fences were cut throughout central and west Texas almost as fast as they were built. The Rangers were called on to do a kind of detective work they had never done before. In 1893 a young county judge, John N. Garner, who was to become Vice-President of the United States, wrote the adjutant general:

> I write at the request of several of the most prominent citizens of this county to inform you of violations of the law in this county and to ask for your assistance.
>
> Francis Smith & Co. some weeks ago fenced their pasture on the Nueces river with a splendid four-wire fence. It had only been up some four weeks when *our entire side* was cut between every post. They rebuilt it at once and in less than ten days it was cut again. They rebuilt it again and last Friday night it was cut a third time. . . .
>
> What we want is about three good Rangers to come here and catch these law breakers. They can catch them in a week or ten days.

[122]

From Brown County came the following:

We have two small pastures near Brownwood. The fences around these pastures have been cut and broken down 50 times during the last five months. We have been notified by letters (signed "White Cappers") that the stock in the pastures would be poisoned. That we would be killed. That our homes would be blown up with dynamite. And that the grass would be burned. The grass has been set on fire three times in the last ten days and a large part burned. We would like to have a man sent here . . . to try and capture the perpetrators. . . . We have been informed that you have the proper kind of men among the Rangers.

From Waller County the governor got a petition from a number of women asking for protection. Of the fence cutters the women said:

They cut our fences and threaten us with death if we dare to repair them. They have overawed the officers of the law who fear to incur their enmity. They have fired shots into the houses of our good citizens at night. . . . They have openly and in the daytime rode up in squads to citizens engaged in repairing cut fences and pushed the muzzles of guns against their persons and threatened them with instant death if they continued their work.

From McCulloch County came this report:

There is in a portion of this county a lawless class of people who cut fences, burn houses, etc. . . . It will take some detective work to get evidence sufficient to punish the guilty and check the lawlessness. We think it advisable for you to quietly send one or two Rangers to go and stay among the lawless element. The local officers cannot find out.

Each of these counties, scattered widely through Texas, was asking for Rangers to work in a new way, secretly, as detectives. Ira Aten, one of the Rangers who tried being a detective, has left an account of his adventures.

Nobody tried harder to catch fence cutters than Sergeant Ira Aten. His efforts began in August, 1888, and extended into October. In August a farm wagon drawn by a horse and mule jolted along a dirt road leading through Navarro County towards Mexia. Two young men clad as farm hands were the occupants. The wagon contained their bedding, some cooking utensils, and a grub box, all in plain sight. The fact that they had six-shooters in the bed rolls, and maybe a couple of Winchesters excited no comment because all travelers went armed in those days.

[123]

The young Rangers turned detectives had to have a reason for stopping in Richland, the heart of the fence-cutting country. They made the reason by pounding a wagon wheel off with an axe. Ira Aten got on the mule and rode into town in search of a blacksmith, who fortunately had gone off on a spree. They dragged the wagon in on three wheels and a pole and went into camp under some trees.

While waiting for the cotton-picking season to open, they got a job repairing a gin. Aten wrote: "We have been working all this week building a rock furnace around the gin boiler. It has been awful hard

work handling the rough and large rocks, but we never grumbled. . . . Jim King says he would not work at it for less than $5 a day only under these circumstances. . . .

"We got to see lots of fence cutters every day. . . . We are slowly getting acquainted with the villains, but it will take a long time to get their confidence. . . . I have heard them say often that their crowd didn't need any help to cut fence and an outfit was a fool to take in any outsiders.

"The fence cutters here are what I would call cowboys, or small cow men that own . . . from 15 head all the way up to perhaps 200 and a few cow ponies. Some have 100 acres of land and some more. . . . They hate Grangers as they call them, for it is the Grangers that have the pastures, with the exception of Frost & Berry and a few others. In fact, they hate anybody that will fence the land either for farming or pasture. They are a hard lot, . . . thieves as well as fence cutters."

Aten did not like the detective business and expressed his dislike thus: "These are my last fence cutters, whether I catch them or not. . . . I would rather be in hell than here. We have had to tell ten thousand lies already, and I know we won't get away without telling a million more. Hereafter it will take more than $50 a month to get me to go out and see how many lies I can tell, or be placed in a position so that I will have to tell them to keep from being murdered. . . . Nothing will do any good here but a first class killing, and I am the little boy to give it to them if they don't let the fence alone. . . . Jim King's fiddle comes in very handy. He draws large crowds very near every night and we make lots (of) new acquaintances by it."

Later Aten reported that the fence on the Love ranch had been cut, and that they were watching every night. "We have a double-barrel shotgun apiece and if the villains cut the fence we are guarding and they don't surrender when called upon somebody will most likely go away with their hand on their belly. I want to take these villains without killing them, but I think a little more of my life than theirs and I will stand trial for murder before I will stand up and be shot (down) like a fool."

In his lonely vigil, Aten's thoughts turned to a better sort of life. "I expect some of these days," he wrote, "to stand up before a fire and shake off my six-shooter and Winchester, kick them in and watch them burn up, and go up in the Panhandle and settle down upon a little farm, go to meeting, be a better boy, and read my Bible more. . . . So

[125]

I don't want to kill these rascals and get any more deadly enemies on my trail than I have already got."

Finally Aten decided it was useless to try to "get in" with the fence cutters or to catch them by "laying on the fence" at night. He climaxed his service with a bold plan to put dynamite under the fence so it would explode if cut. He examined the law to see whether a man had the right to use dynamite in this manner, and found that there was no law prohibiting it. He had bought some dynamite, which he planned to use in the following manner. He would pack it in an old shotgun, tie a string to the bottom of the post and to the trigger. When the fence was cut, the post would fall, pull the trigger, and explode the dynamite. He thought such operation would have to be handled with great care, so as not to blow up the wrong man! "Keep your ears pricked," he wrote, "you may hear my dynamite boom (bomb) clear down there. . . . 1 will use the greatest precaution . . . and see that no innocent man gets hurt with them. They are dangers in setting unless a man is awful careful. However, if I get blowed up, you will know I was doing a good cause."

A Ranger is supposed to have initiative, but Aten had gone too far. The authorities at Austin ordered him to cease and desist, and transferred him to another place. He was quite willing to go, saying he had taught the fence men how to use the bombs and they could dynamite their own fences. There is no record that his invention was ever used, but for years the rumor persisted that certain pasture fences were dangerous to monkey with.

OPERATIONS AROUND EL PASO

Farther west, in the Trans-Pecos and around El Paso, the Rangers were operating singly and in groups. The following report in the records is signed by Corporal C. H. Fusselman. It may be called the story of the now deceased.

"Yesterday morning (June 4, 1889) while in discharge of my duty . . . killed one Mexican name Donaciano Beslanga. I will explain. . . .

"Sunday eve as I rode into Alpine I met Capt. Gillespie, who had a telegram from Haymond station stating that now deceased had the town terrorized . . . had shot one man . . . and was riding through town shooting . . . well, we took 8:52 train and when we arrived . . . the now deceased had gone to Maxan Springs. Got a handcar and went down but did not find him. Returned on 3:20 train. I borrowed a mule and went to Maxan Springs. Found he had left at sunrise. I lay and watched his wife (home) until 10 at night when a heavy storm blew up which drove the now deceased into his home for shelter. I run on him but he slipped me as it was so dark. As I was looking under tank for him lightning flashed and he shot at me. . . . I run towards him and returned the shot. . . . I lost him as it was raining so hard and was so dark.

"Next morning I got a rifle and took his trail at daylight. . . . I heard him cough. I went towards him. . . . He saw me and sprang to his knees. I could see that there was no chance for his giving up as he had a bad expression on his face. . . . I fired as he did . . . the two shots so near together that they could just be distinguished.

"Then about 15 shots were exchanged. . . . I emptied my gun, ran on him, grabbed his gun and shot him once with pistol. . . . I wired Gillespie, who came at night with Justice and held inquest. . . . Excuse this long explanation."

In September, 1891, Captain Frank Jones in El Paso heard that the Southern Pacific passenger train had been robbed in Val Verde County. Horses and men were loaded on a boxcar and were soon at the scene of the robbery. Captain Jones made the following report:

"I followed the trail to the Rio Grande that evening and tied up our horses without any grass at all. The next morning as soon as it was light enough I found where they had crossed into Mexico. There were five of them shod all around. They took a southeast course for about ten miles and then all scattered. They came together, burned a lot of papers, and unshod their horses. The trail led back to the river, recrossed to this side, and again scattered.

"On the fifth day we found where they had reshod their horses. . . . On the sixth day we found their camp in a dense cane brake on the Mexican side. . . . Some dogs came out to meet us. We . . . scattered and tried to look through the cane brake . . . but it was too dense and . . . very dangerous. I set fire to it and . . . closed in as it burned. We located the camp . . . but the men had mounted fresh horses and fled. There was a lot of plunder and three extra saddles of men that had been murdered. . . . We found a great many stolen cattle there and letters that prove they were regulars in the business. . . . I demolished their roost. . . . I spent three days in beating and burning out the brakes on both sides but failed to catch them."

In a flood on the Rio Grande in 1854, the river changed its course and transferred a section of land from the Mexican to the Texas side of the river. This cut-off portion of Mexico became a sort of no-man's land, and a refuge for lawless characters. It came to be known as Pirate Island.

The leading figure on Pirate Island had been Clato Oliguin. He had grown old, but his leadership and reputation had descended to his three sons, Jesus Maria, Antonio, and Pedro. In 1893 Jesus Maria and his son were indicted for cattle theft. Deputy Sheriff R. E. Bryant was sent to arrest them, but the outlaws were too much for him, and an appeal was made for Texas Rangers.

When General Mabry ordered Captain Frank Jones to the region,

the captain wrote: "If I am sent back to El Paso, I hope you can allow me to take more than four men. Old 'residenters' say that four men will simply be murdered and do no good. There must be fully fifty men in the gang that has caused so much trouble. They are part of the mob that murdered Howard some years ago."

When Captain Jones moved against Pirate Island six weeks after he wrote the letter, he had four Rangers and a deputy sheriff. As they approached the Oliguin ranch, they found Old Clato, too old now to fight, and the women and children. They later saw two Mexicans, and pursued them as they fled to some houses in which they took refuge. As the Rangers charged up to the houses and dismounted, a bullet struck Captain Jones in the leg, and another struck him in the heart. None of the Mexicans were killed or captured, but Jesus Maria Oliguin and his son were wounded, and later were captured by Mexican authorities.

The death of Captain Jones left Company D without an officer, and Sergeant John R. Hughes was sent from Alpine to take charge. In time he became one of the prominent Ranger captains.

CAPTAIN HUGHES AND THE HORSE THIEVES

Late in September, 1896, several armed men saddled horses and a packmule unloaded from a passenger train in Alpine. It was Captain John R. Hughes and his Rangers who had come from El Paso to engage in a horse-thief hunt. They were joined by a man named McCombs, who had lost a race horse; Jim Stroud, who had a fine stallion missing; and Deputy Sheriff Jim Pool.

On September 27 the trail of the thieves was found where it led out of the Glass Mountains and into the McCutcheon pasture. There Ranger Thalis Cook and a cowboy found the thieves barricaded on a mountain. Cook pinned them down and sent for help. What happened was reported by Captain Hughes:

"We ran our horses almost to the top of the mountain when the fight was so hot that we dismounted. Here McCombs got a bullet through the ear. We drove them off the mountain top to the side, where two of them were killed."

The Rangers recovered five horses, including the race horse and the stallion. The McCutcheon Ranch provided a buckboard in which the two dead men were hauled to Fort Davis and, in the words of the Ranger captain, "given a decent burial."

In a gunfight such as this incidents often happen which get little notice at the time but form the topic of camp conversation long after. Here is Captain Hughes's report of such an incident:

"When we were saddling up at the Ranch," he said, "a pale-looking man came to the fence and said that if he had a horse he would go with us. I offered him a horse and told him to come on. He could only find a pistol, and I did not try to find him a gun, as he looked like he was not able to carry one." (Note the distinction the Rangers made in their weapons. A revolver was in their official language a pistol, and the rifle was a gun. In conversation they usually called the pistol a six-shooter.)

Captain Hughes continues his story of the invalid:

"When we made the charge on the mountain, he was right with us, and using his pistol. When the heat of the fight was over I looked and saw the boy by my side *with a gun.*

"I asked where he got the gun and he said he got it from 'that man,' pointing to a dead man.

"I asked him if he had plenty of cartridges. He said he had not, but (that) there was a belt full on the dead man.

"I told him to get them. He did so and returned to me and asked me what to do.

"After everything was over I asked who the boy was and learned his name was Arthur McMaster. He had been sick and was staying at the McCuthen's ranch."

Arthur McMaster could no doubt have had a Ranger commission as soon as his health would permit. He had the stuff that a good Texas Ranger was made of.

In 1896 Bob Fitzsimmons was heavyweight champion of the world and Pete Maher was the contender. A promoter named Dan Stuart thought it would be a good thing to have the two big men meet in El Paso. Since nobody had attempted to hold a prize fight in Texas, there was some uncertainty as to whether the law could prevent it. Most of the people of Texas were opposed to prize fights, and Governor Charles A. Culberson announced that there would be none. He instructed General W. H. Mabry to use the entire Ranger force if necessary to prevent it. Four companies—commanded by J. H. Rogers, J. A. Brooks, John R. Hughes, and W. H. (Bill) McDonald—were sent to El Paso. The Rangers found El Paso swarming with ring followers, gamblers, thugs, and western gunmen, the most famous of the latter being Bat Masterson of New Mexico.

The promoters went ahead with their plans. When they found they could not fight in Texas, they planned to move across the line into New Mexico, then a territory, but the territorial authorities would not permit it. Then they thought they could hold it in Juarez, but Mexico would not permit that. The promoters finally decided to go to Langtry, Texas, cross the Rio Grande at that point into Mexico, and hold the fight before the Mexican authorities could reach the place chosen. So they loaded prize fighters, paraphernalia, gunmen, and gamblers on the train and headed for Langtry, where Roy Bean, "the Law West of the Pecos," dispensed bad law and worse whiskey from the Jersey Lily Saloon. The Rangers followed the caravan, but could do nothing to stop the fight, as they had no authority in Mexico. The fight was held, and Fitzsimmons kept the championship.

There is a story about Langtry which has gone into Ranger legend. It may be true, but whether it is or not it shows the influence the Rangers had.

When the fight train arrived in Langtry, an enormous rowdy crowd poured into the Jersey Saloon and into a little restaurant where a pig-tailed Chinaman was the only waiter. He could not possibly serve all the customers. Bat Masterson, sitting near Bill McDonald of the Rangers, became impatient and began to abuse the Chinese waiter. Finally Masterson picked up a pepper sauce castor as if to hit the waiter.

"Don't do that," said Captain McDonald quietly.

Bat Masterson, king of gunfighters, was not accustomed to interference. He looked down at the slight figure of the man beside him with a scowl that had withered bigger men.

"Maybe you'd like to take it up," he said.

Captain Bill, with a faraway look in his eyes, said in his softest voice, "I done took it up."

There it was, the showdown. But nothing came of it. The bad man from New Mexico chose to let it pass, and so another legend about the Rangers was born.

All the incidents which have been described in this chapter show one thing: That a profound change had come about in Texas in this period and that this change was reflected in the duties of the Texas Rangers. The organization was no longer close-knit, as it had been under Major Jones. Excepting occasional trouble along the Mexican border, the Rangers were now dealing with citizens, albeit bad ones, and were subjected to more criticism than they had been earlier. This criticism resulted in the abolition of the Frontier Battalion and a reorganization of the Texas Rangers.

CHAPTER XX

TWENTIETH CENTURY RANGERS: REVOLUTION, PROHIBITION AND WORLD WAR

HE Frontier Battalion was abolished in 1901. The real reason for its passing was that the frontier was gone. It had become an interior police force. The Rangers were operating against citizens of the state and often in competition with local officers, and in doing this they met opposition. The criminals hired lawyers, and some lawyer took the pains to read the law creating the Frontier Battalion. The law said that "each *officer* of the battalion . . . shall have all the powers of a peace officer." The law said that it was the duty of each *officer* to execute criminal processes and make arrests. What about *privates* in the Ranger force? Nothing was said about them. The question was referred to the attorney-general and he ruled, May 26, 1900, that noncommissioned officers and privates in the Frontier Battalion had no right to make arrests or serve legal papers!

A year later, July 8, 1901, a new Ranger force was created. Under the new law, each Ranger was considered an officer and was given the right to perform all duties exercised by any other peace officer. There were to be four companies of twenty men each. Fortunately there was little change in personnel. The four captains had long been in service— John R. Hughes, J. H. Rogers, J. A. Brooks, and W. H. (Bill) McDonald. The distribution of the companies is worth noting; they were stationed either in far West Texas or along the Mexican border. Captain Hughes remained at El Paso; Captain Brooks made headquarters at Alice, near the Lower Rio Grande; Captain Rogers was at Fort Hancock in Hudspeth county, below El Paso and near the border; and Captain McDonald had all northwest Texas, including the Panhandle.

The activities of the new force were similar to those of the Frontier Battalion after 1880. The Rangers hurried to trouble spots where the local officers were unable or unwilling to curb the lawless element. Captain Brooks' men caught a cow thief on the King Ranch, and killed another caught branding a calf. Ranger W. E. Roebuck was killed from ambush, six men were arrested for this crime, and a mob began to form to lynch them. Captain Brooks now protected the prisoners from the mob. "My men are crack shots," he wrote, "and I am not afraid of them getting the worst of anything." Ranger A. Y. Baker killed one of the cow thieves after he had been released on bond, and later a witness for Baker was murdered. Captain Brooks kept the situation in hand, but so much bitterness had been stirred up that he and his men were transferred to another area.

Brownsville, the town that Cortinas had taken in 1859, again attracted attention. On July 28, 1906, some Negro troops were sent to Fort Brown, and several clashes occurred between them and the citizens. On the night of August 13, they rioted, seized weapons from the arsenal, advanced on the town, fired into houses, killed a bartender, wounded the chief of police, and killed his horse. Then they hastily returned to the fort, replaced their guns, and were in bed before the officers could get dressed. The raid was over in a few minutes. The Texas Rangers, among them Captain Bill McDonald, were sent to Brownsville but arrived too late. Captain McDonald, always a showman, did a good deal of talking about what he would do to the United States army. He so impressed one newspaper reporter as to lead him to write that "Bill McDonald would charge Hell with a bucket of water." The identity of the Negro rioters could never be determined, but the matter was settled when President Theodore Roosevelt discharged three companies.

By 1910 the four captains who had taken charge of the Ranger force in 1901 had resigned, completing the break between the nineteenth and twentieth centuries. After 1910 events of great magnitude moved into Texas and cast the Rangers in a new role.

In 1910 the first of a long series of revolutions broke out in Mexico and extended across the Rio Grande into Texas.

In 1917 the United States went to war with Germany and her allies.

In 1917 the great West Texas oil field was opened at Ranger, marking the beginning of the wildest oil booms ever known on this continent.

In 1918 Texas adopted prohibition, the United States passed the eighteenth (Prohibition) amendment, and national prohibition went into effect January 17, 1920.

These Four Horsemen—Revolution, Prohibition, World War and Oil Booms—all loose at the same time, rode down law and order, gave free rein to license, and made demands on the Texas Rangers which they could not meet. The Mexican revolution filled the Mexican border with raiders; the world war filled it with spies, conspirators, and saboteurs; Prohibition filled it with smugglers and bootleggers, with enough left over to cover the state; and the oil booms made West Texas a gathering place for adventurers, gamblers, and murderers.

[135]

Though there were still good men in the Ranger force, there is no doubt that it had deteriorated. The force had become political, because the captains were appointed by the governors, and each new governor appointed a new set of captains. It so happened that Texas had some bad governors in that period, one of whom was impeached, and bad governors appointed bad men, as well as incompetents, as Rangers.

It would take a volume to tell what went on in the period from 1915 to 1925. All that can be done here is to relate a few incidents as samples.

REVOLUTIONISTS AND TRAIN WRECKS

On October 18, 1915, a group of revolutionists from Mexico wrecked a passenger train north of Brownsville. Judge John Klieber, who was on the train, described what happened:

"I noticed that the train began to bump. . . . I felt it slacken speed. . . . It listed to one side, . . . stopped. Scattering shots and then irregular volleys broke out and increased in volume; and cries, shots—'Viva Carranza.' they cried. 'Viva Luis de la Rosa! Viva Ancieto Pizana!'

"It was a warm night and the windows were up, . . . and everyone went to the floor—went in between the seats. You could hear bullets whistling through the car.

"I could hear the bandits getting aboard and passing to and fro. . . . I saw Brashear stick his head into the aisle. . . . I saw a look of intense terror come into his face. . . . I saw the mouth of a rifle go by, and I saw the flash, and I saw blood spurt, and he fell. . . . Finally . . . the blood had come down in a pool and I was covered with blood. . . ."

The bandits killed the engineer, a doctor and a soldier, and wounded two others. They robbed the passengers and even took their shoes which were very scarce among the bandits.

The Brite Ranch, in Presidio County about twenty-five miles from the border, lies in the Big Bend of the Rio Grande, one of the most thinly inhabited portions of Texas. Christmas had come—the Christmas of 1917—and ex-Ranger Sam Neill and his wife were at the Ranch to spend Christmas with their son, Van Neill. The five children were sent to bed early, and the women, as the ex-Ranger told it, "fixed up their little old Christmas tree." What happened Christmas morning is given in Sam Neill's own words.

"Well, . . . the women folks claimed they wanted to get up early. . . . I have always been an early riser, and I got up and went into the kitchen . . . and started me a pot of coffee. . . . I came back into my son's room to make a fire. They had no kindling. . . . I take a basket and went to the woodpile . . . and got the kindling and made the fire. I went back to the woodpile and got other kindling and made one in my wife's room. We were then surrounded by those fellows, but I didn't know.

"When I got back to the kitchen the coffee was ready. . . . I turned from the stove and set in the window drinking the coffee, when I looked down the Candelaria Road, coming from the river, and I saw six men abreast, riding fast. . . . As they come around two big circular tanks . . . I saw them reach and draw their guns. I dropped the cup and saucer and ran through his (the son's) room. . . . He was still in bed; I hollered and said: 'We are surrounded by bandits and have got to fight.' I doubled in my wife's room and got a gun and six-shooter. . . . And as I got out in the corner of the yard, this Mexican . . . jerked his horse up, and he hollered at his men to kill all the Americans. And as he said it, I shot, and he didn't . . . holler no more. . . . When he hollered that, they jumped from behind the walls and tank dumps like a bunch of quail flushed from behind adobe walls. . . . When the shot was fired it sounded like it busted. . . . I thought so . . . from the way the bullets were whizzing. . . . I got in only three shots until I was knocked down."

The bandits took the horses from the ranch and then turned their attention to the Brite Ranch store. While they were looting it, the stage arrived with two Mexican passengers. The raiders killed the passengers, hung the driver, Mickey Welch, to a rafter, cut his throat, tied their dead and wounded on horses, and set out for the river.

This raid was supposedly led by Chico Cano, who had his headquarters across the river from Pilares and El Pourvenir. Chico was a bold leader with a long record. On January 23, 1913, Customs Inspector Joe Sitters, accompanied by Rangers, and other officers captured Chico and started out of the mountains, but Chico's gang waylaid the party, killed Jack, wounded Sitters and a man named Howard, and rescued their leader. Chico swore revenge and got it three years later, May 24, 1916. Inspector Sitters, Ranger Eugene Hulen, and three others were attacked. Hulen and Sitters were killed and all the horses were captured, but not the pack mules. The three survivors rode out barebacked on the pack mules to give the alarm. A party was organized to

go back and recover the bodies. The dead men were found in the canyon, stripped of all their clothing and badly mutilated. Sitters had eleven bullets in his body. The bodies were wrapped in blankets and carried out of the mountains on pack mules. The Brite Ranch raid came in the following year, as related.

By this time the character of the inhabitants of Pilares and El Pourvenir was well known. Of them E. W. Nevill said: "They were not Carranzistas, they were not Villistas [named after two of the Mexican political leaders], they were not anything; . . . whoever is in charge on the border . . . they are with."

Their services to the revolutionists were described by John Pool: "The Mexicans who live in small settlements along the river have no means of livelihood and do not own land or stock and only have small patches in corn as an excuse for remaining on the river. . . . (They) act as spies and informers for the thieves and bandits from the Mexican side of the river, and . . . furnish information to the desperate characters in . . . Mexico and lead them to our ranches."

Raymond Fitzgerald gave this opinion of the El Pourvenir citizens: "Their standing as thieves, informers, spies, and murderers has been well known in this section for two years. They use this El Pourvenir ranch as headquarters, . . . but stayed in Mexico during the day. . . . Several of these people were cousins to the noted Chico Cano bunch of bandits." Perhaps the best indication of conditions in El Pourvenir was to be found in the case of the American school teacher who had gone native, but still had his troubles. He said the Rangers killed his patrons, the wolves ate his goats, the hawks caught his chickens, and a Mexican ran off with his wife.

Captain J. M. Fox was sent into this region in 1917, and pursued a course that brought criticism on the Rangers. After the Brite Ranch raid, a party of eight Rangers under Bud Weaver, accompanied by John Pool, Raymond Fitzgerald—whom we have met—and two other citizens went to El Pourvenir in the night, rounded up twenty-five men, and found Joe Sitters' saddle and merchandise from the Brite Ranch store. "Some shooting started," and Weaver reported that the party withdrew without learning whether any Mexicans were killed. John Pool was more specific: "I do not know," he said, "whether we killed anyone or not, but it was reported that there were about fifteen dead Mexicans there the next morning." He named eight of them, but Chico Cano was not among the dead.

THE PLAN OF SAN DIEGO

With the opening of the first World War spies and conspirators from Germany and even Japan hastened to take advantage of the revolutionary conditions on the border. The result was one of the most fantastic schemes ever hatched in this country. In 1915 a deputy sheriff of Cameron County arrested at McAllen a Mexican named Basilio Ramos Garcia, who had on his person papers revealing what came to be known as the Plan of San Diego. By this plan, the Mexicans with the aid of Germany and Japan, were to revolt and take Texas and the whole Southwest to California from the United States. A part of this territory was to be given to the "downtrodden Mexicans," and the balance to the Negroes, so that two buffer states could be set up in American territory. Nobody was to be enlisted in the army except Mexicans, Negroes, and Japanese. The war was to start February 15, 1915, to be waged

against what one conspirator called "the damned big-footed creatures of the north," and "the white-faced hogs of Pennsylvania." The war was to be without mercy. All American property was to be confiscated, and all American males over sixteen were to be killed.

Though the plan was fantastic, it created consternation among the scattered ranches of the border. Lon C. Hill reported what amounted to a modern-day runaway scrape. He said the Americans were going north, the Mexicans going south, and the country people were moving into the towns for safety.

"They brought their women and children into town, and a great many just got on the train and left, left their chickens and hogs and cows, and everything else, and just went to Corpus and San Antonio, and went from there to Canada—just scattered all over the country."

"What were the objects of the raids?" asked the investigator.

"That was a question that bothered us. . . . What were they up to? Now, when the thing first started we couldn't understand . . . why those fellows . . . would want to come over . . . and steal a few cows. . . . We got to investigating . . . and we found out that they had been sending a lot of money through the post office . . . to a firm known as Magnon Bros. . . . and they would order guns and ammunition. . . . It got . . . noised around . . . that they were trying to take that country . . . and they said they were going to run all the Gringos out of there.

"Well, that was absolutely inconceivable . . . how a bunch of Mexicans would take a fool idea in their heads that they were going to kill all those Americans and take that country. . . . But they were coming . . . they would tell us . . . coming . . . in bunches and take your horses and burn up your houses and kill you and then . . . they were just going to come over in a great big army and take the whole country. . . .

"We would get hold of some fellow . . . and ask . . . what in the name of goodness is the matter with you Mexicans; are you all going crazy here? What are you up to; what are you going to do?

" 'Well,' they said, 'we have organized, and we have got some foreigners going to help us, and we are going to take all the land back that you Gringos stole from us before the constitution of 1857.' "

The Texans, supported in some instances by the Rangers, inaugurated a sort of reign of terror among the Mexican population. Many excesses were committed, and there is no doubt that innocent Mexicans were killed. There was murder on both sides, for such is the nature of war. If the Mexicans cried "Kill the Gringos," the Americans replied "Kill the Greasers." There is no doubt that the Texas Rangers and with them the citizens killed innocent Mexicans during these times.

The excesses committed finally led to an investigation of the Texas Rangers by the Texas legislature. This investigation was initiated by J. T. Canales of Brownsville, a Texas citizen of Mexican blood and a kinsman of Cortinas. In justice it must be said that the Texas Ranger force had deteriorated. Some governors appointed men because they had political influence, and not because they were men of character and intelligence. J. T. Canales was right in saying that the Ranger force "was honeycombed with undesirable characters and in great need of reorganization." The investigation began January 31, 1919, and lasted nearly two months. The Rangers were charged with the murder of prisoners and other offenses. The Ranger force, which had been much enlarged, was cut back to four companies of not more than fifteen men, and in addition a captain and sergeant were named for each company.

CHAPTER XXI

FRANK HAMER—A MODERN RANGER

CAPTAIN FRANK HAMER has been called the last Texas Ranger of the old tradition. He may not be the last, but he is perhaps the best known among those whose service fell wholly in this century. We know more about his early life, how he became a Ranger, and the minute details of his activities than of any of the others. The story of his rise to fame shows clearly the character and training of these men.

Frank Hamer was born near Fairview, Wilson County, Texas on March 17, 1884, but his parents moved to San Saba County when he was six years old. This move put Frank in the Hill Country of Texas, where settlers were few, game plentiful, and where there was still opportunity for a boy to live in the open by running streams and amidst the alternating prairies and woodland. It was the sort of country that suited this boy. Schools were short and vacations long, an arrangement also to a boy's liking.

In school he read Wilbarger's *Indian Depredations,* which dwelt on the wild and ferocious nature of the Indians, especially the Comanches, and it emphasized the suffering and heroism of the early settlers. But in the book Frank Hamer read of men who lived close to nature, who understood it. "I made up my mind," he said, "to be as much like an Indian as I could." This did not mean that he wanted to be cruel or scalp people, but that he wanted to live in the woods, find his own food, and make friends with all the animals. He set out to do this, and fortunately his mother was not one of those women who believed in keeping a small boy under her feet.

Frank began excursions into the country from which the Indians had but recently retired. His trips became longer, extending over days and finally to a week or two. He took his gun, ammunition, some fishing line and hooks, and some matches, maybe a little salt, though he may have gone without salt as the Comanches did. He got acquainted with the wild creatures. The flight of birds told him where water was to be found, and their cries often indicated where he could look for the wildcat or the wolf. He learned the different tracks and how to follow them. He began imitating animals and birds, and could do this so well that they would come to him if he would remain motionless like a stump. He could call up crows, quail, deer, road-runners, fox-squirrels, and the hoot owl. Since he lived on game, he became an expert marksman and learned early how to handle all sorts of firearms. He also learned how to handle a knife and how to throw it so accurately that he could kill game in this way. It is doubtful if any Indian ever had keener eyesight. Frank Hamer's vision was such that he could see a bullet in flight, not the actual pellet but a small vapor cloud that a bullet makes whizzing through the air. His sense of hearing and sense of smell were equally keen.

Frank Hamer learned as a boy how to ride a horse and to care for one. At the time he grew up everybody rode horses, and San Saba County was a good horse country. He loved to tell about the good horses he had known, what fine companions they were on lonely trips, and how the horse and the rider come to understand each other. By the time he was grown, he knew many of the things that a Texas Ranger of those days had to know. He had become a woodsman, trailer, marksman, and observer of all that went on around him, either in nature or among men.

At seventeen Frank Hamer was six feet two, with an inch to grow, slender, wiry, and strong. He became a cowboy on the ranches. An incident occurred at this stage which indicated that he had courage. He was on some mission that took him into strange country, and brought him to a village where a number of tough characters had gathered. The young stranger had on good clothes, fine boots, and an expensive hat, better clothes than the tough characters were accustomed to seeing. They began to haze him, to talk of taking his boots, hat, and shirt.

One of them advanced on young Hamer as if to begin stripping him. Frank drew out his knife and opened it. When the bully got very close,

Frank Hamer spat full in his face. For a tense moment it was a question of whether the man would accept this insult or tackle the youth with the knife and fire in his eyes. The insult was accepted, and the boy got on his horse and rode slowly away.

Many a boy in West Texas wanted to be a Texas Ranger. Each man who became one has a story to tell about how he qualified for the service. The captain of the company selected his own men, recruiting them from young ranch hands and peace officers. The two qualifications which made a good Ranger, and eventually an officer, were unflinching courage, guided by unerring judgment, and an intelligent awareness of all that went on around him. But how did the captain of the Rangers learn about men who had these qualities? Here is the way Captain J. H. Rogers found out about the cowboy Frank Hamer.

It was Sunday at the Carr Ranch in 1906. It was a lonely Sunday because Frank Hamer was the only person at the ranch house. Telephones were new then, and everybody was on the party line listening to the conversations being carried on in the ranch country between Fort Stockton and Sheffield. Frank Hamer heard a sheriff call a former deputy and ask him to catch a horse thief headed that way. The former officer declined, saying that he had other things to do. Hamer broke into the conversation and told the sheriff that he would capture the thief when he stopped at the Carr Ranch for water.

"Who are you?" asked the sheriff.

"I am Frank Hamer and am working at the Carr Ranch."

"Well," said the sheriff, "if you catch him, that will be fine. I will describe him."

"No need to; I heard you describe him."

Hamer figured that the horse thief would reach the Carr Ranch in the early morning hours. He got up at three o'clock, and, taking his rifle and six-shooter, he concealed himself near the windmill. The horseman showed up about daylight, and rode straight to the water trough—straight into the muzzle of Frank Hamer's Winchester. He disarmed the man and started him back the way he had come to meet the sheriff. In describing his feeling later, he said: "I sure felt good going up and down the long slopes with that thief ahead of me." He rode sixteen miles before he met the sheriff, who was coming in a buggy drawn by two fast-stepping horses. On the way back, the sheriff asked

Frank how he would like to join the Texas Rangers. He said he knew Captain Rogers and would speak to the captain about the Carr Ranch cowboy. Frank Hamer enlisted as a Texas Ranger on April 21, 1906. He was twenty-two years old. His service in the Ranger force was not continuous, but he always returned to it when there was great need.

FRANK HAMER'S CAREER

It would not be possible to relate all of his varied experiences and adventures. The following incidents are only samples of the sort of life

he led, and of the sort of life the Texas Rangers led during this century.

In the last chapter we saw something of conditions along the Mexican border, inflamed by world war and revolutionists. Frank Hamer was a member of Captain W. W. Taylor's company during a part of this trouble. In the lower Rio Grande Valley there was a Mexican bootlegger named Delgado who had a permit to drive a cart between Brownsville and Matamoros during the day, but at night he was a smuggler of opium, mescal, and tequilla. As a cart man he was peaceful enough, but as a night smuggler he was desperate and dangerous. The officers learned that on a certain night Delgado would cross the river at a certain place and follow a trail leading into Texas. The officers concealed themselves near the trail. Their orders were that they should call on anyone who approached to halt, and to shoot only if the order were disobeyed. Hamer objected, saying that Delgado was dangerous and would kill someone if he had warning.

"I am in favor of giving him the works first and the orders afterwards."

"We might kill an innocent man," his officer said.

"No, we won't kill an innocent man, because no innocent man is going to be on this trail at this time of night." Hamer was overruled.

As the Rangers rode through the night to the place, Hamer noticed that his friend, Delbert Timberlake, had a shotgun. Hamer thought he should have brought a rifle and told him so. Timberlake seemed to have a premonition of what was going to happen to him that night. He said that the kind of gun he carried made little difference. "I'll get mine any way you take it."

Waiting by the trail, the Rangers heard the bleat of a goat, the Mexican's signal. As the man came up the trail the officers could hear the brush scratching his boots. When the figure came in range, the officers gave the command "Halt." Delgado fired instantly; the single bullet hit the ground, richocheted and wounded Timberlake fatally. Hamer fired with the Winchester, so rapidly that the gun looked like a pear burner. Delgado ran a few feet and fell with two Winchester bullets in his body.

Hamer was bitter over the manner of Timberlake's death. The officers took him to a Brownsville hospital, where he died the next day. Hamer was with him at the last.

"Pancho," he said, "there's not a chance for me, is there?"

"No, Tim, there's not a chance for you."

"Did he get away?" asked Timberlake.

"No."

"That helps a lot," said the wounded man. Then he was gone, and the living man pulled a sheet over the dead one and went to join the waiting officers outside.

"Hamer," said one of them, "if we had followed your advice, things would have been different. We made a mistake."

"Yes," said the Ranger, nodding to the white sheet that could be seen through the window, "and there is your mistake."

From January 1, 1922, to November 1, 1932, Frank Hamer was Captain of Headquarters Company, stationed in Austin. This meant that he was the senior captain and had some supervision over the entire force. In this interval he conducted cleanup campaigns in the oil-boom towns from Ranger, the first, to Borger and Kilgore, which were towards the last. He helped police the Red River during the dispute between Texas and Oklahoma over the boundary; and he solved a number of murder cases. Much of his time was taken up in enforcing Prohibition, a duty that no Ranger liked. It was in 1928, however, that he performed a service outstanding in the history of any law-enforcement body. This performance has been called Hamer's war on the Texas Bankers' Association.

In 1927–28 there were a great many bank robberies in Texas and the Southwest. The bankers got very tired of these robberies, and they decided to stop them by offering a reward for dead bank bandits. Signs were posted in the banks:

REWARD
FIVE THOUSAND DOLLARS FOR DEAD BANK ROBBERS
NOT ONE CENT FOR LIVE ONES

Following this, so many were killed that Captain Hamer became suspicious and began to wonder if they were real bank robbers who were being killed. After careful study, he came to the conclusion that innocent boys, weaklings who were half drunk, were being "planted" at the banks and shot down by officers and others who received the five-thousand-dollar reward and divided the money among all who were in the plot. In short, a murder machine had been set up in Texas. Frank Hamer decided that he would break it up.

He explained his suspicions to the bankers, but they would not withdraw the rewards. He went before grand juries but could not get indictments against the officers, because they controlled the courts in the counties where they lived and where the murders were committed.

He seemed to be at his wits' end. There was, however, a chance to appeal to all the people by telling the whole story to the public.

On March 11, 1928, Captain Hamer gave a prepared statement to the press, and the next day every large newspaper of the state spread the sensational revelation on the front page. *The Dallas News* headline read:

> Victims "Framed" to Collect Robber Rewards, Says Ranger Hamer
> Hamer Claims Full Proof of "Murder Ring."

The San Antonio Express had this lead:

> Robber Reward Killings Framed, Ranger Charges
> Murder Machine Already Pockets Part of Bounties
> Paid for Dead Bank Bandits, Hamer Says.

The prepared statement read in part as follows:

"The purpose of this article is to lay before the people of Texas, and the bankers of Texas, certain facts that they ought to have about the dead bandits and the rewards that have been paid for them. I agree that bank robbing should be stopped. . . . But I do not agree that the method adopted by the Bankers' Association of Texas is either wise or just, because it is adding the crime of murder to the crime of robbery.

"There has come into existence in this state a murder machine. . . . Here are the conditions . . . out of which this machine sprang. . . . The first . . . is that bank-robbing had become widespread. . . . There is a group of criminals who make bank-robbing a profession.

"A group of bankers . . . offer a reward of $5000 for dead bank bandits. For one taken alive they would not pay a cent. This reward has aroused the greed and desire of a small group of men who have more love for money than for human life. . . . There is another group of men—usually young men, drifters, and loafers—whose principal traits of character are weakness combined with a reckless spirit. These are the men who are lured by the unscrupulous ones mentioned above into bank robbery only to be shot to death by officers. . . .

"Here is as perfect murder machine as can be devised. . . . If what I have said is true, . . . then the situation that has come about in this state is a disgrace to Texas and to civilization, and should not be tolerated."

Captain Hamer then gave proof he had collected to show that innocent men had been murdered for the reward, and that other murders were being planned. He challenged the bankers to appoint a committee to which he would submit the proof he had, and he appealed to the people and the peace officers to help in stopping organized murder.

His appeal was effective. In a few days the grand juries indicted men for murder, and the Texas Bankers withdrew or modified the reward they had been offering. It required a great deal of courage to conduct a single-handed campaign directed against the wealthiest class in the state. When this was called to his attention, Hamer replied: "When you go fishing, what kind of fish do you like to catch, little ones or big ones? The bigger they are, the better I like to catch them."

CLYDE BARROW AND BONNIE PARKER

Captain Frank Hamer's most famous case was probably his pursuit of Clyde Barrow and Bonnie Parker. At the time he rendered this service he was not a Texas Ranger, having left the service two years previous, in 1932. The story begins on January 16, 1934, between daylight and sunup, when four prisoners were delivered by unknown parties from Eastham Prison Farm near Huntsville, Texas. One prison guard was killed, and the others held off by men hidden in the brush with machine guns. The prison delivery had been carried out by Clyde Barrow and one or two others. The officers all over the state were alerted, but Clyde Barrow could not be captured.

On April 1, two state highway patrolmen saw a strange car parked on the roadside near Grapevine. As they went to investigate, they were shot to death by a dark-haired man and a red-headed woman, Clyde Barrow and Bonnie Parker. By this time the number of murders committed by these ruthless killers numbered fourteen, and was soon increased to fifteen. Clyde and Bonnie never gave an officer a chance, but shot on sight. They lived in an automobile, and made a circuit covering three or four states—Texas, Oklahoma, and Louisiana constituting their principal range. They were never still long at a time, and would

[151]

often cover a thousand miles in twenty-four hours. They had committed so many crimes that they were now desperate and determined not to be taken alive.

Lee Simmons, superintendent of the Texas State penitentiary, decided to put Frank Hamer on the trail of the two killers. Hamer was given the proper credentials and set out on the tough mission, alone.

He took the trail February 10, 1934, and followed it to where it ended near Ruston, Louisiana, on May 23. Captain Hamer had never seen either the man or woman he was after, but he interviewed many who knew them. He came to know them even to what clothes they wore, what cigarettes they smoked, and what kind of cars they like to steal and use. He knew that Bonnie carried a pet rabbit and fed it lettuce. He followed them for 102 days.

The Ranger finally learned where their "post office" was, a dead stump beside the road near Ruston, Louisiana, where they left and received letters from their friends and confederates. Finally, he learned that Clyde and Bonnie would visit this post office early on the morning of May 23. In the meantime another Ranger, B. M. Gault, joined Hamer, and for the appointment with Barrow at the post office four other officers from Texas and Louisiana were called in. The six men concealed themselves in the pines near the road opposite the stump post office. The officers reached the place at 2:30 in the morning and constructed a blind out of pine branches. About seven o'clock a car showed up; it contained a dark-haired man and a red-headed woman. It came to a stop near the pine stump, and when the two occupants looked toward the dead stump, Hamer ordered them to surrender, knowing that they would never do it. When they reached for their weapons, the officers fired. Clyde Barrow's foot released the brake, and the car rolled slowly into the shallow barrow pit at the side of the road. The car was riddled with bullets and both occupants were dead.

The car contained three automatic rifles, two sawed-off shotguns, nine Colt automatic pistols, one Colt revolver, one hundred machine-gun clips of twenty cartridges each, and three thousand rounds of other ammunition. Thus did the former Texas Ranger bring to an end the careers of two merciless killers. Frank Hamer had made the transition from the days when both officer and outlaw went on horseback to the time when both used automobiles and traveled a thousand miles a day.